Poems for Movement

A Teachers' Anthology

EDITED BY

E. J. M. WOODLAND, B.A. L.R.A.M. L.G.S.M.

PRINCIPAL LECTURER, HEAD OF THE

ENGLISH DEPARTMENT, BOROUGH ROAD COLLEGE

Evans

EVANS BROTHERS LIMITED, LONDON

Published by
EVANS BROTHERS LIMITED
Montague House, Russell Square, London, W.C.1

This collection © Evans Brothers Limited 1966

First published 1966
Reprinted 1967
Reprinted 1970
Reprinted 1973

Set in 10 point Baskerville
Printed in Great Britain by C. Tinling & Co., Ltd.,
London and Prescot

ISBN 0 237 28124 4   PRA 3729

CONTENTS

ACKNOWLEDGEMENTS

The Editor and publishers are indebted to the following for permission to use copyright material in this book: Messrs. George G. Harrap & Co. Ltd., for lines from *At Night in the Wood*, originally published in "Rhymes for Wee Woodlanders"; Mrs. N. R. Hawes for *Snow Maidens* and *Creeping Jenny*; Mr. A. G. Prys-Jones for *The Princess Wai*; Miss H. I. Rostron for *So Silently* and *Close Your Fingers*; Mrs. Rita Spurr for *Cement Mixer*; Miss Kate Stevens for *The Chestnut Trees*, *Washing Day* and *Postman Bold*; and the Editor of *Child Education*, in whose journal all the above poems and many others in this book have appeared.

Every effort has been made to trace the owners of copyright but the publishers take this opportunity of tendering their apologies to any whose rights may have been unwittingly infringed.

PREFACE

The collection of verses in this book was made following experimental work undertaken with Infant Group Students of Hockerill College and comprises poems written by them, together with others originally published in *Child Education*. The many headmistresses and teachers who have already shown interest in our work—which may be described as "poetry and movement" for children from 5 to 8 years old—suggest that others may also welcome a collection of this sort. The concept of "music and movement" is already familiar, that of "poetry and movement" rather less so. The article that follows indicates some of the principles on which it is based and the experiences we were seeking to provide for the children.

I should like to thank all the contributors to this anthology for their work, and those schools which have been so generous in making time, facilities and children available for our experimental work. The students taking part met with enthusiasm and responsiveness from the children; nevertheless, their co-operation and unselfishness in giving time to writing, experimenting and reporting deserves the warmest acknowledgement. I should like also to thank the Principal and staff of Hockerill College, who were so generous with their interest and encouragement.

E.J.M.W.

POETRY AND MOVEMENT

"Poetry and movement" is the name given to an interesting and effective method used as part of physical education with young children; this book provides for teachers a selection of material to be used for this purpose. The work is not intended to replace "music and movement", where the aim is to teach music and movement together. Here, as many people think, imagery properly has no part in the early stages; to deal with music, movement *and* imagery is just too difficult for very young children. However, imagery and movement do go happily together, with sense, sound and rhythm stimulating pleasure in movement. Teachers know how much children enjoy listening to poems. The verses collected in this book are pleasurable to hear in themselves, but have also been chosen with the elements of good movement work in mind. The teacher will find that they invite the children to respond to movement, and can be used singly as part of a lesson or in groups to make up a whole lesson.

Few teachers can now doubt the importance of movement work in the whole education of the child, for it is both a skill and a means of expression. All physical education in the Infant School sets out to develop the children's bodily powers and to give them confidence and skill in their use. To achieve this, the children must come to know the parts of the body and their relation to each other and to the whole. Movement work provides the opportunity for experiment and practice in acquiring this "body awareness", as it is called. Body awareness and skill in movement are also of the utmost importance when children are attempting creative work. Movement is a means of expression where the child's dawning perceptions of shape, pattern and rhythm, and his love of imitation, fantasy and imagery can be given full play.

The immense importance of movement work is recognised by all authorities and constantly stressed in Colleges of Education and teachers' courses; much time has been spent in investigating the best methods of building up suitable programmes. "Music and movement" is already well known as a combination that helps them both; the movement being induced and extended by the stimulus of music, and the appreciation of musical qualities being encouraged as responses are given bodily expression. Poetry and movement have the same kind of relationship. Poetry, too, promotes enjoyment and experiment in movement and provides the stimulus for much expressive and imaginative work. Since we are much concerned in this book with movement, a restatement of some of the aims and elements accepted by the authorities on the subject may be helpful. It will be easier then to see how the poetry and the movement are related.

In his analysis, Rudolf Laban has shown that every movement has a time element, takes place in space and has a weight element. By time here it is meant that a movement may be short or long, quick or slow. Young children find it easier on the whole to move quickly, not yet having full control and bodily co-ordination. However, movement work should encourage and stimulate the acquiring of these, so provision should be made first for sharp contrasts in quick and slow movements and later for more sustained, controlled slow movement. The latter can also be practised by allowing part of the body to be supported while a slow movement of another part takes place. For example, children curl up very small on the floor and then are encouraged to uncurl very slowly until they are in a stretched position with arms and legs extended; their weight is supported by the floor throughout. Simple relaxation of muscle tension should follow such a movement.

It is sometimes hard for adults to remember just how difficult it is for the five- or six-year old to estimate the space around him. The toddler who constantly insists that he is a big boy "right up to the ceiling" is struggling to relate his own size to his surroundings, and, of course, to assert his own importance. To help children understand and come to terms with the idea of space, we must try to remember how we felt at that age. There are two aspects of space to discover: the space immediately surrounding the child's body and the total space of the room, hall or playground.

First, consider the space immediately surrounding the child's body. It can be divided into that above him, that around the lower part of his body, the space in front and that behind him, and the space on either side of him. Children need to be encouraged to explore and use movement in all of these. They are often taught to face the teacher and tend to make all movements looking one way unless specifically encouraged to venture in other directions. The teacher can help here by changing her position in relation to the

8

group, by moving from place to place in the room, so that the children concentrate on what they are doing and not on carrying out a movement to or for the teacher. In developing the use of this space around the body, the children's love of contrast can be used effectively. They love to be "thin and tall", "fat and squat", "twisted" or "straight". Movements can be high, encouraging children to stretch up, to use their arms above their heads to reach into the space above them; or they can be at medium level, using the space all round the body when it is in a standing position; or they can be low, exploring the space round the child on the floor. For example, he may experiment to see how far his leg will stretch backwards, forwards or sideways, or how small or large a space he can occupy on the floor.

The matter of exploring the total space of the hall is very important, for children need to be confident and happy in their use of the whole area. If they are not encouraged to explore it, their movements will be confined and restricted and will lose in freedom, variety and originality. Very young children will feel much more confident when close to others and will be happiest if allowed to start from close proximity to the teacher. They will enjoy the opportunity in the first few lessons to make short excursions from this place of safety. Some children have been accustomed at home to large gardens and extensive playing areas; others, from flats, maisonettes or houses without gardens, may have experienced only very restricted areas. These children will need much more sympathy and understanding at the outset than the former. The example of other children and their own natural love of freedom of movement, together with the skilful encouragement of the teacher, should soon overcome the timid children's initial hesitancy. At this stage, they must be lured into experiment, not forced to it. A teacher of admission classes will know that the child who has clung to her skirt for three weeks in the classroom before being induced to become independent in the increasingly familiar environment, may return to all his former uncertainties when taken into the hall. This retrogression is understandable, but interest in the movement work going on and a desire to take part in it should soon help to re-establish confidence. It is to encourage this very confidence that movements are designed to use the whole space of the hall and not to use only the space around the child.

The element of weight in movement is fairly self-explanatory, being defined as the degree of tension in the muscles which produce it. A stamping or thrusting movement is heavy or strong, a stroking or fluttering one light. Children soon learn to appreciate the difference between heavy and light and thoroughly enjoy using them in contrast with each other.

Implicit in all that has been said about these three elements of time, space and weight is the need to encourage the body-awareness mentioned before. Adults know by long experience what movements can be expected of or achieved by various parts of the body, though it is surprising how small a range of movement they sometimes have, far less than the total of which a particular part is capable; and with age comes declining muscle tone and increasing restriction. Children have the opposite experience: they do not know what they can expect their bodies to do. Many a child has reached up for a jam-pot far out of range and wept with frustration when he cannot grasp it. This is only one small example of his need to learn. The good movement lesson provides opportunity for the child to experiment in moving all parts of the body, beginning with simple, broad movements of arms, legs, trunk and head and progressing to more and more intricate movements as opportunity, ability and his invention suggest. The lesson is not one in which the child has licence to let off all his surplus energy in unpurposive movement, and not all activity should be vigorous, fast and exhausting. Small, delicate, light movements, using fingers and toes, wrists and elbows, ankles and knees, are just as important and rewarding. The children gain increasing control of their muscles and find satisfaction in extending the range of movements which they can use in interpretative work. The lesson will use the child's powers of concentration to the utmost; this is why it is important also to include moments of partial or complete relaxation.

Movement using the space of the hall, or locomotion, is equally important. At first the children will either walk or run, and there are many different ways of doing these simple things. Soon they will become interested in other possibilities—hopping, skipping, galloping, jumping, leaping and sliding. The more inventive they become and the more confident in their bodily powers, the more unusual become their movements in locomotion. Wriggling, somersaulting, even a primitive version of cartwheeling, may be attempted. Inexperienced teachers are sometimes appalled at the thought of forty children moving at will over a large area. However, the children are just as interested in ways of stopping and enjoy experimenting with the sudden stop or the slow, very gradual cessation of movement. It is easy to use this interest to help the children to stop when required and at a recognised signal. In this movement round the hall, the children are gaining valuable experience in estimating their own position and speed in relation to that of other children. The tumbles and collisions of the Nursery School soon give place to the speed, dexterity and grace of most Junior School children. If a child appears to be abnormally slow in making these adjustments, there may be some physical factor such as poor eyesight or poor muscle development to account for it; this should be investigated. Assuming that the picture is of gradually increasing confidence and skill, the child develops awareness of others about him and, while the teacher should not force the situation, she can begin to provide opportunities for the children to combine together in movement. This may be group movement, as the children become autumn leaves fluttering together or waves of the sea or horses pulling a coach, or it may occur when two or three children join together quite spontaneously as their purposes for the movement coincide. They may break away or gather up others quite freely; and this freedom is essential.

Shape and pattern in movement are important. The body of the child can be made to assume different shapes. It can be outspread or rolled into a tight ball; it can be long and slender; it can be round and squat. In changing from one to the other, a pattern of movement is traced. This patterning can be, as it were, two-dimensional when the child's body remains on the same plane of movement and he traces a pattern in progression on the floor —for example, a circle. Triangles, squares, straight, wavering or jagged lines can be "stepped" out. The patterning becomes three-dimensional when it is combined with the changing shape of the mover, so that a more subtle pattern is made. These patterns can be very simple at first and, as the children gain in control and expressiveness, they will become more complex. At first the child will work on his own, making his own movements without bothering about what others are doing. Later he may see the possibilities of extending his range by combining with someone else. A simple example is where two children join hands and do the same movement together. Later, all kinds of development can take place; for example, one child may stand still while another moves in relation to him, both can approach and recede and so on. Children will probably enjoy having some simple shapes or patterns suggested to them by the teacher; this can be done through discussion, but the children must remain entirely free to use the suggestions or not as they feel able at the time.

At the outset, it is best to let the children experiment with their movement, concentrating all their mental energies on its demands. It is astonishing how quickly their imagination begins to work and then, provided interpretation in movement is left completely free, suggestions of possible subjects can stimulate and maintain interest in the work. For example, children can be asked to move like a big, heavy, clumsy bear or hop like brisk, gay sparrows. We cannot remind ourselves too often that there is no "right" or "wrong" way to move, only the way the child feels to be necessary. They can, in other lessons, be encouraged to look at the way things move, their shape and weight, their stiffness or suppleness. Their attention can be drawn to the differences in the ways people move; for example, the marching soldier, the coalman with a heavy sack, a lame woman and so on. In the movement lessons, these and hundreds more can be used to lead on to simple characterisation, mime and group work.

Before leaving this discussion of the nature and aims of the work it must be stressed that movement is not only a skill in itself but also a means of expression. Some children do not readily put their ideas into words—whether orally or on paper. Perhaps these children have a compensating skill in drawing and painting and can express the ideas they are struggling to tell in this way. Some children have no outstanding skill, and indeed may have less than average ability in both these means, but it does not follow that they have nothing to "say". Teachers who watch children doing movement work will often see that a child slower in acquiring other means of expression has become articulate, even fluent, in free movement where he can show what he feels or sees, or even give form to the vivid products of his imagination. It does not follow that a child without expressive ability in words or paint *will* have it in movement, but it is a possibility. Moreover, most children thoroughly enjoy acquiring a new means of expression and a new dimension in which to experiment and develop.

Before going on to see what help verse can give in promoting good movement work, it would be well to examine some of the qualities that poems intended for use with young children should have. Firstly, however simple the themes and subjects appear, they should be carefully considered by the teacher. They must be within the child's grasp and experience. Sometimes a poem looks simple on the page; it may have short lines and easy rhymes but, if it has an idea too difficult for the children to understand or an emotion too complex, it is doubtful whether it should be used. In these circumstances, the appreciation can only be partial and many children will be bewildered or bored. It is surprising, again, how much verse offered to children is concerned with customs, situations, even people who have disappeared from our society. Poems about maying or lamp-lighting, muffin men or crossing sweepers, mean little or nothing to the five- to eight-year old. Children's emotions should be sincere, not falsely sentimental when aroused, and the verses should stimulate responses which are not imitative reflections of adult sentiment. Subjects for children's poems readily suggest themselves from their environment. The weather, the seasons, animals, toys and amusements, the people around them, all are endless sources of interest. There is also a place for fantasy and imagination. If the stimulus is vivid, vital and not falsely sentimental, then children can thoroughly enjoy a poem which begins "Just supposing" or "Let's pretend". The poems in this anthology, in addition to providing a strong stimulus to movement, have been carefully selected to indicate those subjects and themes that make a special appeal to the present-day child in the Infant School.

So far, we have been concerned with the subject-matter of the poems, but children rightly demand much more of what is given them. We can nearly all recall the wonderful fascination of a new word or phrase, the meaning of which was still obscure to us but which felt splendid on the tongue and pleased our ears. Children can be heard chanting such words over and over for the sheer pleasure of their sound. Other words have onomatopoeic effect and produce great satisfaction for that reason. To talk of "crunching" dead leaves, "squelching" slugs or "slithering" over ice exactly expresses the sensation of the action. Children are seeking all the time to extend their repertoire of words, and when they are not provided with sufficient satisfying ones, they either cease to bother or invent their own. It is important, therefore, that poems should have expressive words. As the children can only respond to a reasonable quantity at once, there should be a few good, new words, if possible repeated. Too many together in a poem make it difficult for the child to grasp the meaning. If he finds one or two new words which please him by their sound and newness, he is likely to enjoy and so remember them.

So far the sound of individual words and phrases has been discussed; now we must consider their effect when taken together. Children have a wonderful sense of rhythm, and repetitive sounds with a satisfying rhythm, even when they carry no meaning, are a delight. Quite young children make up chants of sound sequences for themselves and jog or bounce in time to them. (That the enjoyment persists for adults is shown by the popularity of nonsense chorus lines in ballads and shanties.) Here the rhythm gives the pleasure. Poems for children should therefore offer clear, enjoyable rhythms, though the metre need not always be strictly regular, beat and stress being more important than the exact counting of syllables to the line. Most poems for children have a simple line and stanza structure in which the pleasure of rhyme also plays its part. Finally, the poems should give a sense of completion in subject-matter, development and form. At this stage, they should be completely satisfying: the witches should return home after their night ride, the story sequence have its end.

The poems in this collection have been chosen because they show these varied qualities and give pleasure in these ways. Children enjoy hearing the teacher speak or read them, and will remember them without difficulty.

As we have already said, however, they also have a more specialised purpose, and it is possible now to examine the part they can play in movement lessons. Some of these will take place in a large room or hall, others in the classroom. Ideally, all should be given where there is plenty of space; in practice, with so many claims on the hall, some will have to be held in restricted areas, Most of the poems can be used under any conditions, though they will be treated differently according to the situation.

Let us consider them first in large spaces. We have seen that movement classes are used to develop the child's ability to experience space, size, time, weight and shape, and most teachers are familiar with the part music can play. Poetry can be used in much the same way. Poems such as those about snowflakes or autumn leaves in the wind will encourage the child to explore and use the space of the hall as well as that immediately around him. Others, such as *Polishing*, suggest contrasts between high and low, or, as in *Samson Fullength*, contrasts in size. A poem like *Trees* needs space so that shape and body movement may be combined, while the idea of weight with progression is part of *Giants and Fairies*. Suggestions for variation in speed in repetitive action, as in *Lightly, Lightly*, are very numerous. Some of the poems call for complete relaxation— with plenty of room to lie down—while many others, such as *White Horses*, begin or end in relaxation. Some obviously suggest the use of particular parts of the body, and encourage play with fingers, toes, hands and arms. Others demand whole body movements or progressive, repetitive, rhythmic movement.

Here, a detailed discussion of a few poems will clarify what may be expected from them. The little poem, *Lazy-bones*, begins with the children curled up on the floor. Stanza 1 leaves time for them to assume the position and enjoy holding it. In stanza 2 a slow, stretching movement begins in toes and legs. In stanza 3 head and trunk movement begins and as the child imagines the cold air he tenses muscles to meet it. Next he stretches hands and arms over his head and holds the whole position stiffly but briefly. Finally, he relaxes completely and is brought to his feet ready for the teacher to pass on to the next movement activity. The whole stretching movement is a slow one and is therefore supported throughout, the child's weight being borne by the floor.

The Willows starts with the children standing stiffly and still. Some children will suggest the shape of the tree, others will not attempt this. This position is held through the first two lines, and then gentle, light, fluttering movements begin in the hands and arms and an easy swaying movement of the trunk and head. The children are encouraged by the last two lines to bend forward while continuing the gentle movement. This poem helps the children to think about and remember the shape of the trees and the kind of movements they make, so that they can attempt the appropriate movements themselves. They need room for this but no progression takes place. The word "forlornly" will probably have to be explained and the suggestion that it carries of "being alone" should prevent the children from bunching together for their work. As this poem keeps the children in one place, it is a good one to precede such a poem as *Playing at Circuses*. Here the children will move about freely, imitating the actions of the ponies and clowns. *The Willows* could be the starting point for building up a more extensive movement picture. The children suggest movements of other trees, flowers and grasses. The whole class can try these out and there should be a good variety in interpretation. The gentle, rippling movements of the stream can be added. Some children can then be asked to represent the willows, others new plants, yet others the stream. The hall becomes a meadow and the children take an active interest in building up a simple movement picture of it. This poem could also be used in a fairly small space if it were given a different treatment, as it does not call for vigorous progressive movement.

A poem such as *Skipping Susan* obviously gives opportunities for various kinds of movement, either on the spot or in locomotion. Stanza 1 gives a fine skipping movement which the children may have seen expertly carried out by older children. Here they practise it without any fear of being tripped by the rope. Stanza 2 gives another vigorous hopping movement which is succeeded in stanza 3 by a stretching movement. By its very nature, it brings the class to a standstill. The last stanza gives a gentle, whole body relaxation for the children's muscles and quietens them effectively after the earlier excitement. The whole poem offers a change from brisk activity to steady stretching, followed by relaxation.

The *Rag and Bone Man* gives an opportunity for quite simple characterisation. Here the children are asked to recall what they may have seen of such a character. Their love of imitation and role-playing is here given an outlet and the actual movement suggestions by the teacher are kept to a minimum. *Jenny* takes the characterisation further, and a clear sequence of actions is suggested for the child to perform, ending again in relaxation. In *The Baker*, there are at least three characters present. Younger children are likely to play just one, or else all three in turn. Older children may join together in groups of three, each child playing one role. The same aims and elements which underlie the movement suggested in other poems are maintained here, but such poems of characterisation and fantasy lead on quite naturally to spontaneous drama. This is always unscripted but may or may not have words. Once young children have become absorbed in an idea of a character or sequence of happenings, they delight in

16

acting them out. A script would be a positive disadvantage, for the endeavour to remember exact words inhibits naturalness of interpretation, producing stereotyped actions and making the whole proceeding a memory test instead of a genuine, fully experienced piece of creative activity. If the children feel the need of words, they will use them.

Many a playlet has grown out of a poem such as *Golly*, where this favourite character performs antics to amuse the other toys. It is not long before the children begin to suggest a variety of appropriate movements for other toys to make; fairy dolls, balls, engines, aeroplanes and many more will soon be mentioned. A whole toyshop of activity can be built up.

Many teachers like to group all the work of their children both in and out of the classroom round a topic or theme, recognising the great importance of not making the child's day a fragmented sequence of unrelated experiences, and knowing that learning best takes place when ideas and experiences are associated together. The wall-stories, paintings, writing activities and told stories all follow such general themes as "The Circus", "Toys", "At the seaside", or nature topics such as "Spring", "Birds" or even "Hibernation". Many of the poems in this anthology are especially suitable for this kind of work, providing opportunities for the expression and use of information acquired in the course of classroom work on many individual themes; and the poems have been arranged in sections not only to cater for this "topic approach", but also to suggest the wide range and variety that it can take.

Just as the classroom work can be extended in the hall, so the vivid experience of a poem and its movement in this unrestricted space may stimulate work when the children return to the classroom. Some children may wish to write about it, others may attempt to draw characters, scenes or incidents that they have met in their poetry. Topic work of this kind requires much time to organise: suitable poems are not always easy to find and supplementary material does not come readily to hand, while much poetry that is otherwise suitable for children offers no opportunities for "movement" anyway. And yet the more the children enjoy this type of work, the greater the need for material. This anthology, bringing together a wide and varied range of "movement" poetry in convenient form, is designed to save the long and sometimes fruitless search that teachers have often hitherto faced.

A whole lesson in the hall may be built around the poems, as long as a careful selection is made to allow for a great variety of body movements that will give opportunities to acquire skill and do creative expressive work. Such a lesson may begin with a poem like *Marching at Night*, the children sitting and listening while the teacher first reads it through. Then, when she repeats, the children should move vigorously and rhythmically, using all the space of the hall. This may be followed by a whole body movement, for which a poem like *Rowing* would be very suitable. The children will now have worked hard at two quite strenuous, large movements, so that a finger or toe dexterity poem would be a good choice to follow next. With the children seated round her in a group on the floor, the teacher could read *Quack, Quack*, or a similar poem, and then go on to a poem asking for very vigorous progression, like *Wild Horses*. This should be followed by one calling for relaxation, such as *Summer Day*, and the twenty-minute lesson could end by more extended work on one poem related to the classroom topic and perhaps calling for sequence or characterisation. Here, with the children grouped about her, the teacher can recall in a few words what the children have already discovered or heard about the subject before she reads the poem. It is a good idea to read the poem twice before the children move, once so that they may take in the subject and savour its expression, and the second time so that they may begin to respond to the movement suggestions. When the children are ready to make their first attempts, each finds a space to stand or sit, so that the class is distributed over the hall; when the arms are raised sideways or forwards, no child should be touching another. The teacher will now say the poem again as expressively as possible, keeping an appropriate pace and rhythm. The more naturally and flexibly she speaks, the better the children will respond and the fewer the specific suggestions for movement she will need to elicit from them. She will watch the class and praise concentrated effort, taking care, however, to avoid encouraging children merely to imitate; each child should be free to develop his own interpretation. If some movement in the poem is not very well done by all, she can ask the children to show her how each one thinks it should be done. This gives the slower or less able a little practice before coming back to the poem again. How the lesson proceeds from here will depend on the age and experience of the children.

Little ones will have concentrated on it long enough by this time. Older children may be ready to combine in a group movement based on it or to build up a simple mime or playlet.

Children love to return to old favourites, and these should be included from time to time among the new material. In the whole scheme of poetry and movement work, care must be taken that all the elements already outlined are catered for. Not all can be practised in each lesson, but a balance should be preserved between dexterity movements, whole body movements, progression and relaxation. A proper balance must be provided, too, between work on skills and creative, expressive work.

Some teachers may prefer to use the poems just as part of a movement lesson in which recorded music, percussion instruments, piano, etc., may all be used. As these do not just accompany movement but give insight into the relationship between music and movement, so poetry is an integral part of the movement experience and has its place in these lessons. Simple poems and simple tunes have many things in common: they have a time or duration element; they have rhythms that may be fast or slow, even or jerky; they have sounds that are pleasing or evocative; they are capable within themselves of contrasts in speeds and, as simple harmonies are pleasing to the children's ears, so is the sound of the words. Some teachers who do not themselves play an instrument or have access to a suitable collection of records will find these poems of considerable help in supplementing their resources of material to stimulate movement. Movement to poetry may be included as a part of every lesson.

So far the emphasis has been on work in a large hall, but the poems may also be used in the classroom, when the exigencies of the timetable make lessons necessary there. Finger dexterity poems, those for other parts of the body and, indeed, any that do not call for vigorous progressive movement can be used. Many such poems, about trees and flowers, for example, are included in this anthology; others lead on to mime and spontaneous drama, two activities very suitable for the classroom. Here the suggestions for the initial characterisations and sequences of actions, found in Sections VI and VII, will quickly engage the children's interest and provide convenient starting-points for the work.

The poems in this anthology have been grouped under topic

headings, so that the teacher may quickly find rhymes for every purpose. This has the further advantage, when the teacher is looking for material in the appropriate section, of suggesting how her work may be developed and extended. Some teachers will wish to be able to select verses to stimulate certain kinds of movement, and an index, under appropriate headings, has been provided for this purpose. Many poems appear under more than one heading, as they may be used in more than one way; in fact, it must be emphasised that more than one treatment or interpretation is frequently possible and there is no question of one being *right* and the other *wrong*. However, for those who so far have had little experience of this type of work, brief notes have been appended to certain poems, where the movement implications are less immediately obvious, or where it may be helpful to show the elements of movement included. The notes appear in each of the topic sections, though there are fewer for poems of action sequence, characterisation and fantasy. Here, the movement is often actually described in the poem itself, and in any case the interpretation is best left to the children. In the earlier sections, where it is sometimes more difficult to see just how a poem can be used, the suggestions offered are more numerous.

Every teacher will realise that, as the children's experience in this type of work grows, their responses to any poem will become more and more varied. These will reflect their increasing skill in body control, their developing imaginative powers and their growing interest in the subject. This, indeed, is the main purpose of "poetry and movement", the thing that we are really seeking to encourage. The teacher will recognise that the children must not rely on her to suggest responses once they have overcome their initial uncertainty; this is only an indication that she is not using the method effectively. Ideally, the responses will soon become individual and often delightfully unpredictable as each child develops his own powers of perception and expression. Moreover, the relationship between each teacher and her class is a highly personal one and it is rarely possible to anticipate which poems will be most successful or which will cause most difficulty for any particular group. Much depends on the teacher's understanding of the needs of her class and her enthusiasm for the work; as long as these are present, class and teacher alike will enjoy to the full the experience of "poetry and movement".

LIST OF POEMS AND AUTHORS

* Indicates poems for which notes and suggestions have been made.
† Indicates poems contributed by students of Hockerill College.

SECTION I

WEATHER, SEASONS, COUNTRY AND SEASIDE

SECTION II

MOSTLY FLOWERS AND TREES

SECTION III

ANIMALS: BEASTS, INSECTS AND BIRDS

SECTION IV

THINGS TO DO

24

SECTION V

BUSY DAYS

SECTION VI

PEOPLE

SECTION VII

PLAY, FANTASY AND MAGIC

SECTION I

WEATHER, SEASONS, COUNTRY AND SEASIDE

WHERE WAS FEBRUARY?

On January the thirty-first
Everyone was worried—
Where was February?
Everybody hurried,
—Up to the market,
Down through the town:
"Please find February,
The reward is half-a-crown."
That night,
At midnight,
With everyone in bed—
Sly old February
Slowly showed his head.

LINES I TO 8 Children bustle about looking for February, asking each other where February is or announcing the reward.

LINES 9 TO 11 Children lie down and go to sleep.

LINES 12 AND 13 One child slowly stretches and stands up.

FOUR WINDS

North Wind is boisterous,
   His voice rough and shrill;
He drives the wild snow-storms
   Over the hill.

South Wind is dreamy,
   He murmurs his song,
In tree tops, in grasses,
   All summer long.

East Wind is cruel,
   Bears sleet on his wings;
He waves a keen whip
   That lashes and stings.

West Wind is gentle,
   Refreshes the flowers;
He comes from the ocean
   And brings warm showers.

WILD MARCH WIND

Wild March wind came out to play,
    He scampered here and there,
Snatched off my hat and tugged my scarf,
    And tangled up my hair.

I chased my hat all down the lane,
    And wild March wind chased me,
Until I found it safe and sound—
    'Twas hanging from a tree.

My legs are tired, I'm out of breath,
    I'm tired of such rough play.
Please stop your antics, wild March wind,
    Until another day.

VERSE 1 Children pretend to be out in the wind.

VERSE 2 Children chase hats and then reach up to take them from the tree.

VERSE 3 Children sit down, stretch and relax legs and then rest.

A WINDY DAY

March wind, rampaging down the street
With roaring breath and silent feet!
Whistling, moaning, rumbling, sighing,
Round the houses keyhole spying.
Whining through the chinks and cracks,
Groaning down the chimney stacks.
Ruffling feathers, lifting hats,
Scattering dust and rumpling cats,
Whisking clouds across the sky,
Billowing sheets hung out to dry,
Confusing cock upon the steeple,
Laughing loud at all the people!
Wise folk shake their heads and mumble:
"He must have his rough and tumble!"
But wait a while and we shall see
What a lamb he's going to be!

THE SONG OF THE WIND

Out in the meadow
The grasses blow,
To and fro, to and fro.

Out on the ocean
The waves leap high,
Toss and fly, toss and fly.

Over the sky
The white clouds chase
In silent race, in silent race.

And I, the wind, am their
Master proud,—
The Master of grass and wave
And cloud.

I rush and I swirl
I twist and I twirl,
I blow and I laugh with glee.
And the grass and the waves
And the clouds are tossed,
Bent and lifted and scattered and tossed
And all by me, by me!

FLAGS

See the flags, straight and stiff,
On their masts so high.
Now they flutter in the breeze,
Waving to the sky.
Limp and floppy down they fall
When there is no breeze at all.

LINES 1 AND 2 Children stand with arms stretched out stiffly.
LINES 3 AND 4 Children wave arms gently as in a breeze.
LINES 5 AND 6 Children allow arms to fall to their sides limply.
N.B. Children may be reminded that their bodies are the tall, straight masts.

WINDMILLS

The wind blows high,
The wind blows low,
And round and round the windmills go.

Slowly, slowly,
To and fro,
Then faster and faster, round they go.

VERSE 1 Children wave their arms in circular motion to imitate sails of a windmill.
VERSE 2 Children follow changes of pace suggested by the words.

THE RAINY DAY

'Twas such a cold and windy day,
The rain was splashing down,
It rained upon our window pane,
It rained upon the town.

I looked and hoped for hours and hours,
But still it did not stop.
It kept on splashing, splashing, splashing,
Plip, plop-plip, plop-plip, plop!

But then the sun began to shine,
And all was bright and gay;
The flowers peeped up to say hello,
And greet the sparkling day.

GARDEN IN THE RAIN

I sat beside the window,
Nose flat against the pane,
And stared out at the garden
All misty in the rain.

No animals were stirring,
No sunlight could I see.
The garden, wet and gloomy,
Seemed a horrid place to me.

That cannot be my garden
Indignantly I cried,
Perhaps the rain is crying
Because my garden died.

PUDDLES

There are large puddles, small puddles,
All made by the rain,
Brown puddles, black puddles,
Puddles in the lane,
Puddles we step over,
Puddles we jump through,
Cold puddles, warm puddles,
Muddy puddles too.

There are puddles by the wayside,
Puddles in the field,
Puddles gaily shining
Like a soldier's glinting shield.
Puddles that go splash,
Puddles that go splosh.
Puddles here so deep
We need a mackintosh.

THE RAIN

Pitter-patter, pitter-patter,
Little drops of rain,
Pitter-patter, pitter-patter
On the window pane.

Pitter-patter, pitter-patter,
Little drops of rain
Gently falling.   Gently falling
To the ground again.

Pitter-patter, pitter-patter,
Little drops of rain
Running quickly.   Running quickly,
Dance into a chain.

Here the children may imitate the rain-drops.

VERSE 1 With head, arms and hands the children suggest the rain-drops dashing against the window-pane and trickling down.

VERSE 2 Arms and hands move gently downward. A whole body movement to the ground follows.

VERSE 3 Here the children use the suggestion of running, then join hands to suggest the rain-drops running together into trickles.

SOUNDS OF SPRING

Listen! Listen! What can you hear?
Was it a mouse that came pattering near?
    Was it the wind that blew in the trees?
Or flowers that swayed in the rustling breeze?

Was it a bird that flapped in the sky?
Or was it a deer that went leaping by?
    Perhaps it was flowers blossoming near?
Listen! Listen! What did you hear?

That was a squirrel scampering there.
A fox goes by and skulks to his lair.
    That was a song of a calling bird.
Those were the sounds of spring we heard.

IN SPRING

My garden looks so pretty
Now that spring is here.
The flowers open slowly,
Their colours bright appear.

Emerging from the darkness
Dull and brown and dank,
They lift their heads up shyly,
From hedge, from bed, from bank.

The sun shines in the daytime,
The petals open wide.
They stretch their heads like giants
And leaves spring from each side.

When darkness creeps upon them
Each coloured flower, it's said,
Closes up so softly
And the flowers go to bed.

Children arrange themselves in groups to suggest flower-beds.

VERSE 1 Children lie curled up and then very slowly begin to uncurl.

VERSE 2 Gradually the children rise from the floor, keeping their hands and arms folded over their heads.

VERSE 3 Children use hands and arms to show the open flowers.

VERSE 4 Children relax hands and arms. They stand with heads drooping and bodies bent forward a little.

SUMMER AFTERNOONS

A sleepy time, a dreamy time,
These summer noonday hours;
When drowsy bees hum in the lime
And in the clover flowers.

The wind sounds sleepy in the grass,
And in each leafy tree;
While lazily the white clouds pass
Above the dreaming sea.

The birds are silent that were gay;
Idle the butterflies;
And cattle stand through half the day
In ponds, with half shut eyes.

Throughout the poem children lie relaxed, as in the warmth of
the sun.

ROWING

Swing the long oar
through the drifting water
See the waves breaking
in furls as we falter.
Curved is the blade
like the curve of a bow.
Swing your arms backwards
and forwards we go.

WEATHER WISE

When I go home from the seaside,
What shall I take with me?
Pebbles, or shells, or seaweed:
Tell me, now, which shall it be?

Pebbles are smooth for feeling,
Shells get broken, I fear;
But seaweed, like satin-smooth ribbon,
Will last for the rest of the year.

Seaweed, like satin-smooth ribbon,
Will hang by my window pane,
And tell me, in weather-wise language,
Whenever it's going to rain.

So when I go home from the seaside,
I know which one it will be;
I'll take the satin-smooth seaweed
To remind me of days by the sea.

WHITE HORSES

When the sky is calm and the air is still,
    And the wind lies fast asleep,
The little white horses of the sea
    Are dreaming in caverns deep.

Then the wind awakes; his voice rings clear
    With an echo loud and long,
The horses stir in the ocean depths
    For they love the sound of his song.

And up they float through the water green
  To the curve of the shining bay,
And the glad wind whistles a welcome shrill
  As they hurry to frolic and play.

The little white horses rear and prance
  And their foaming manes stream free,
As faster and faster they gallop apace
  To the tune of the wind and the sea.

They stamp and leap, and their pounding hooves
  Make thunder wherever they fly,
As they race the clouds and the screaming gulls
  In the wild and stormy sky.

Then the wind grows tired; his voice is faint
  As he softly whispers, "Go"—,
And down the little white horses plunge
  To the quiet depths below.

And they sink to rest in their caverns cool,
  To dream in the blue-green haze
Of the scurrying clouds and the gulls' harsh cry,
  And the glory of stormy days.

VERSE 1 Children lie on the floor relaxed.

VERSE 2 Children begin to listen and stir.

VERSE 3 Children rise with a smooth, stretching motion and prepare themselves to move off.

VERSES 4 AND 5 They imitate horses, gradually increasing speed.

VERSE 6 Children's movements become gentler as they prepare to relax.

VERSE 7 Children return to total relaxation.

SEA HORSES

Sea horses, sea horses,
Wildly they ride,
Foaming and free
With the running tide.
White manes tossing
High in the air,
Prancing away
To their deep sea lair.
Sea horses, sea horses,
Plunge 'neath the waves
To your echoing home
In the ocean caves.

THE SONG OF THE WAVES

We are the quiet, timid waves that gently
    kiss your toe.
We hardly seem to move at all, so softly do
    we flow.
The only sound we ever make is a whisper or
    a sigh,
But inch by inch we creep along until the
    tide is high.

We are the jolly, bubbling waves that laugh and
    splash with glee.
We bustle up the seashore, as merry as can be.
We spill our foam upon the beach, spread like a
    soapy pool,
Then slide back quickly to the sea and leave the
    hot sand cool.

We are the heavy, roaring waves, that burst in
    clouds of spray.
We crash against the cliff-side, and swirl and
    spin away.
As each of us falls backwards, there's another
    close behind
To hammer at the sturdy rock; to smash and tear
    and grind.

VERSE 1 Children make soft, flowing movements with hands, arms and whole bodies, while gently moving forward.

VERSE 2 Children use brisk, sharp movements of hands, arms and legs. They move forward to suggest the waves breaking.

VERSE 3 Here really strong, vigorous movements should be made with all parts of the body.

N.B. It helps to suggest that one end of the room represents the beach.

THE MERMAIDS' SONG

Gold of the sand and blue of the sky,
Green of the sea when the waves rise high,
White of the foam and the seagull's wing,
This is the song the mermaids sing.

Sharp cold sting of the salt sea spray,
Tide-washed shore at the break of day,
Smugglers' cave where the echoes ring,
This is the song the mermaids sing.

AT THE SEASIDE

I like to paddle in the sea,
To dig the yellow sand.
I like to look for tiny shells
And listen to the band.

I like to walk along the beach
And watch the seagulls fly.
I like the wind that blows my kite
Away up in the sky.

But best of all, when in my bed
Quiet and still I keep,
I like to listen to the waves
That lull me off to sleep.

FUN AT THE SEA

Down to the seaside let us go.
Down to the sea we will dash.
We will put in one finger and we will put in
                                    one toe,
And then we'll go in with a splash.

We'll take out a foot and give it a shake,
We will shake our fingers too.
Let's jump up and down to keep ourselves
                                    warm
In the sea of green and blue.

SONG FOR THE SEASIDE

Sun bright,
Sands white,
Rocks drying,
Pools lying . . .

Boys and girls with bare feet wet,
Swinging bucket, dragging net,
Run from pool to pool to find
What the sea has left behind.

Weeds all leathery,
Weeds all feathery,
Weeds like whips to send friends hopping,
Weeds with bubbles ready for popping.

Jellyfish, starfish,
Shrimps and crawfish,
Flowers in the water like the flowers of the ground,
Crabs that scuttle the long way round,
Drifts of shells,
Strange salt smells . . .

Boys and girls with bare feet wet,
Swinging bucket, dragging net,
Run from pool to pool to find
What the sea has left behind.

Sun bright,
Sands white,
Rocks drying,
Pools lying . . .

THE SHELL

I found a delicate pale pink shell
    On the sandy floor
    Of the ocean's shore.
I picked it up and I listened well
    Till I heard the sea
    Breaking proud and free,
Till I heard the wild waves rise and swell.
    Oh, pretty pink shell,
    Weave your magic spell,
And tales of the sea forever tell!

SEEDS

Seeds that twist and seeds that twirl,
Seeds with wings which spin and whirl;

Seeds that float on thistledown,
Seeds in coats of glossy brown;

Seeds that burst with popping sound
From their pods to reach the ground;

Seeds with hooks that clutch and cling:
Seeds I plant for flowers next spring;

Seeds of every shape and size,
Soon will sleep 'neath winter skies.

MICHAELMAS DAY

Michaelmas Day, Michaelmas Day,
What shall we do on Michaelmas Day?
The corn has been cut,
The birds flown away,—
Nothing to do on Michaelmas Day.

Michaelmas Day, Michaelmas Day.
What shall we do on Michaelmas Day?
Let's make a garland,
All purple and gay.
Michaelmas daisies for Michaelmas Day.

AUTUMN DANCE

Harlequin and Columbine
Are dancing on tiptoes,
   Twisting, twirling,
   Spinning, whirling,
As the wild wind blows.

Harlequin and Columbine,
Flaunting colours gay,
   Stepping lightly,
   Gaily, sprightly,
On an autumn day.

Harlequin and Columbine,
In gold and bronze and red,
   Pirouetting,
   Time forgetting,
Like bright leaves are sped.

AUTUMN LEAVES

O, it's fun to rustle the leaves,
The crispy leaves on the ground,
To ruffle the leaves and scuffle the leaves,
And shuffle the leaves around!

So here I go, and there I go,
Where the leaves are floating down,
The curly leaves, the twirly leaves,
Yellow and red and brown!

And I talk to the wind about the game,
As he goes whistling by,
This gusty game that we can play
The leaves, and the wind and I!

SWEEPING UP THE LEAVES

The Autumn leaves come tumbling down,
Covering the paths outside of town.
Like a brown carpet they cover the ground,
Falling softly without a sound.

Come along children, pull up your sleeves,
Pick up the broom and sweep the leaves.
First to the left and then to the right,
Sweep, sweep with all of your might.

Sweep them into a tidy pile,
Now you may rest for a little while.
We'll make a bonfire as big as can be,
As high as the sky for all to see.

AUTUMN REFLECTIONS

Here they all come, fluttering down,
Crinkled and orange, crunchy and brown,
Crispy and russet in village and town,
To litter the pathways—make gardeners frown.

Scrunchy and yellow, they'll all fall in time,
From the oak and the ash and the elm and the lime.
Small ones and big ones, both narrow and round,
Quickly or slowly they'll sprinkle the ground.

Then they'll be swept in a rickety mound
Waiting for someone to burn them down,
Down, down, down to the ground—
The orange and yellow and russet and brown.

CHASING LEAVES

I'm chasing the leaves on a windy day,
Under the trees and far away;
They rustle and bustle and twirl around,
They scutter and flutter all over the ground.
I'm piling the leaves in a great big heap
To make a warm bed for the seeds asleep.

CLEARING UP THE GARDEN

The autumn leaves have fallen down,
Fallen down, fallen down,
The wind he came and blew them around,
And blew them around.

Let's find a brush and start to sweep,
Start to sweep, start to sweep,
And make them into a great big heap,
Into a great big heap.

Then light the bonfire and burn them away,
Burn them away, burn them away.
And now it's tidy we'll dance and play,
We'll dance and play.

LEAF-FALL

Golden, yellow, brown and red,
Pirouetting overhead.
See them flutter, twist and curl
Dancing in a windblown whirl.
Till upon the ground they lie
With a brittle dying sigh,
Buried in the earth's warm bed,
Wrapped in coats of brown and red.

LINES 1 TO 4 Children dance, using hands and arms to suggest
the movements of the leaves.
LINES 5 TO 8 Children sigh and relax gently.

BONFIRE NIGHT

Watch the fireworks whizzing round,
Round and round along the ground.
Up they go into the sky
High, high, so very high.

Watch the jumping-jack go round,
Round and round along the ground.
Watch the rocket going up,
Mounting skyward, up and up.

Take a sparkler, watch it spark,
Sparkling brightly in the dark.
Watch the fire so burning bright,
Blazing warmly in the night.

Here the children may pretend to watch the various fireworks,
suggesting by their poses and expressions what is happening.
Alternatively the children may themselves be the fireworks and
the fire and represent their movements.

NOVEMBER MIST

Curling and swirling, silent and soft,
Into the cellar and into the loft,
Creeping through keyholes and under the door,
The mists of November are with us once more.

They're cold and they're damp, but they're beautiful too,
And the view from the window seems magic and new,
For the mist's pearl-grey gown each house does enfold
And gives to each street-lamp a halo of gold.

SO SILENTLY

As soft as feathers,
    As quiet as can be,
Something is falling
    So silently.

As white as daisies,
    Down from the skies
Something is flying
    Like butterflies.

As soft as feathers
    It floats to the ground:
Snowflakes are falling
    Without a sound.

MY BRISTLY BROOM

My bristly broom I push and push
To sweep away the snow and slush;
My bristly broom, as tall as me,
Is busy as a broom can be.

My bristly broom can swish and sweep
To clear a path where snow lies deep;
My bristly broom has made a way
For us to skip and slide and play.

My bristly broom now needs a rest
From brushing snow; we've done our best!

MY SNOWMAN

I made a fine big snowman
Beside our garden wall.
When I came back from dinner
He hadn't moved at all.
But when it came to tea-time,
The sun came out to play,
And my fat and jolly snowman
Melted right away.

LINES 1 TO 4 Children stand as snowmen.
LINES 5 TO 8 Children gradually relax to the floor, allowing
arms and hands to droop and bending heads and trunks.

WHEN THE SNOW COMES

Ice is on the pond now,
The sky is cold and grey.
Look! Oh, look! It's snowing,
Let's go out and play!

Make a lot of snowballs,
Roll one on the ground,
See it getting bigger,
Push it round and round.

Now we'll put a head on,
Two eyes, a pipe, a hat.
What a lovely snowman
So white, so tall, so fat!

SNOWFLAKES

See the snowflakes twirling, twisting,
See them dancing all around.
Watch the snowflakes gently falling,
Watch them floating to the ground.

Hear the wind come madly rushing,
Hear it roar along the street.
See the snowflakes blown and scattered,
See them like a great white sheet.

Now the wind is dying slowly,
Now it's peaceful once again.
Now the snowflakes settle gently,
Covering every road and lane.

LET'S BE SNOWFLAKES

Let's be snowflakes
Whirling to the ground.
We make a soft white carpet,
Without a single sound.

Let's be fir trees
Stretching to the sky.
See our branches swaying
As the north wind hurries by.

Let's be Jack Frost,
Busy with his brush.
He leaves a shining pattern
On every tree and bush.

Let's be snowmen,
With hats and scarves so gay.
When Mr. Sun looks down at us
We quickly run away.

Let's be Santa Claus,
With his sack of toys,
Filling stockings to the brim
For lucky girls and boys.

Let's be reindeer,
Pulling Santa's sleigh.
With merry bells a-jingle
We gallop on our way.

VERSE 1 Children weave lightly in and out, then sink softly to the ground.

VERSE 2 Children stretch up, holding out their arms to form branches. One child takes the part of the wind, the others sway from side to side.

VERSE 3 Children pretend to paint patterns on trees.

VERSE 4 Children stand "on the spot" pretending to be the snowmen. One child is the sun. He holds out his arms to form rays. As he shines on the snowmen they run away and hide.

VERSE 5 Children pretend to carry heavy sacks on their backs. They go "from house to house" opening sacks and filling stockings.

VERSE 6 Children choose partners. With hands crossed behind backs they gallop around the room, keeping in step with each other.

When the snow is on the ground
And we make a snowball round,
Then—
I slide.

When the frost is on the trees
And icicles on roof-tops freeze,
Then—
I hide.

When the fires are burning bright
In the hearths on Christmas night,
Then—
I sleep.

But when Father Christmas packs
Jolly toys into my sack,
Then—
I peep!

SANTA CLAUS'S SECRET

What has Santa in his sack
That he carries on his back?
He has toys so bright and gay
All for us on Christmas Day.

Here is a lovely bouncing ball
To play with by the garden wall.

Here's a furry Teddy Bear
With a bright blue bow to wear.

Here's a lovely story book
Inside are some pictures—look!

Here's a pretty baby doll
Wrapped up in a woolly shawl.

With toys like these so bright and gay,
We'll wish you a happy Christmas Day.

As children say this poem they can pretend to look in the sack
and hold up toys.

GOLLY

Golly was a big boy,
As big as big could be,
He loved to walk and strut about
For all the toys to see.

He'd puff and blow, move up and down,
Throw out his chest and joke and clown.
The toys all clapped their hands in glee,
For Golly's tricks were fun to see.

He twisted and danced, he sang a song,
It seemed he could caper the whole night long,
But soon he was weary, worn out with his fun,
His movements grew slower, his playtime was done.

At last he could only just stagger to bed,
Lie down, and lazily lower his head.
But the smile on his face was still shining bright
As he dreamed of more tricks he could do the next night.

A GARLAND OF EVERGREEN

Let's make a garland for Christmas
    Of evergreen tied in a ring,
With berries and baubles and candles;
    Let's twine it with tinselly string.

Let's make a garland for Christmas
    And hang it for people to see,
To wish them the happiest Christmas
    From you and the garland and me.

MISTLETOE

Through the red sun's frosty glow,
In the orchard thick with snow,
Hunting, hunting we will go
For green and silver mistletoe.

Robin whistles clear and gay,
"Follow me—I know the way!
On the apple-tree's bare spray
Mistletoe you'll find today!"

While the grey clouds swiftly blow,
Homeward, homeward now we go,
Crunching through the orchard snow
With our bunch of mistletoe.

AT BETHLEHEM

Silently the shepherds
Came within the stable,
And laid their baby lambs
By His manger cradle.

Humbly Eastern Kings
Knelt within the stable,
And placed their precious things
By His manger cradle.

Holy Angels fair
Kept watch within the stable,
And gazed with loving care
On Christ in manger cradle.

Over the desert
From lands far away,
We have been riding
By night and by day.
Our camels move swiftly,
Their harness bells ring;
A star shines above us
To show us a King.

Gifts we are bringing
To lay at his feet,
Gold for a crown, myrrh,
And frankincense sweet.
We follow the bright star
Which shone for His birth.
This King must be greatest
In all the wide earth.

Move swiftly, tall camels,
Ring, harness bells, ring,
And carry us safely
To worship the king.

SECTION II

MOSTLY FLOWERS AND TREES

SNOW MAIDENS

Like little fallen drops
Of snow,
Fair maidens
In my garden grow.

Each maid
A small green bodice wears,
And in her ballet gown
Appears.

Where chilly winds
Blow cool and sweet,
White maidens
In their dancing meet.

And while they move,
How fine to see
Such petticoat
Embroidery!

DAFFODIL GOLD

At first just tiny tips of green
From 'neath the dark earth can be seen.
Then one by one the blades appear,
Each like a green and living spear.
The sheath which hidden sunshine holds
Bursts, and the golden flower unfolds.
Now like a graceful lady fair,
Daffy-down-dilly is smiling there.
Another lovely tale is told
Of springtime beauty—daffodil gold.

The whole poem suggests an uncurling, upward movement of the
body, with raising of hands and arms.

THE CLOVER FIELD

Who knows the clover field?
The bees, gold-striped and dun,
Working all day in the sun,
They know the clover field.

Who knows the clover field?
Moths that by moonlight hover
On the dewy heads of the clover,
They know the clover field.

Which way to the clover field?
The wind can tell the way,
The wind that blows night and day,
Over the clover field.

HONEYSUCKLE

Gently growing round and round,
    The honeysuckle leaves the ground,
Putting out her tiny shoots,
    Tiny shoots from tiny roots.
Growing up, she does her best
    Until she has to stop and rest,
Drinking in the cool, cool dew,
Drinking 'till she feels like new.
Then on and on, round and round
Until the top can't see the ground.

THE ROSE

A rose woke in the morning sun
And its petals opened one by one.
Smooth and soft and sparkling with dew,
They started to shiver as a cool wind blew.

The wind blew stronger like a gale,
Tearing the petals, so soft and frail,
Until they drifted down and down
And gently fluttered to the ground.

For this poem hands alone could be used.
Children begin with fingers folded over.

LINES 1 TO 3 Children gently stretch their fingers.

LINES 5 AND 6 Stronger movements are made with whole hand.

LINES 7 AND 8 Gentle, fluttering movements are made until hands rest completely relaxed.

SUMMER ROSES

In spring the little rose buds
Are tiny as can be,
They're waiting for the sunshine
To make them grow for me.

Now June is here, they open wide,
Their colour all aglow—
Red and pink and yellow,
Or white as winter snow.

The summer wind blows gently,
Their petals softly fall.
Let's put them in our baskets,
For their scent is best of all.

THE DANDELION CLOCK

I picked a dandelion clock
And held it near my nose;
I blew the pretty fluff away,
And counted up my blows.

"It's one o' clock, it's two o' clock,"
I gave a great big puff.
"It's three o' clock, it's four o' clock,"—
Away went all the fluff.

My dandelion clock was right,
For mother called to me,
"Come in and wash your grubby hands,
It's nearly time for tea."

THE HAY MEADOW

Yesterday the grasses
Stood tall and thick and green;
They swayed in summer breezes,
And field-flowers grew between.

Tall buttercup, moon-daisy,
Sweet clover, red and white,
All grew in summer sunshine,
And drank the dew at night.

Grasses and meadow flowers,
Their brief, bright day is done,
Cut down by the mower,
They wither in the sun.

Down in the broad green meadow,
Where we saw the grasses sway,
The evening breezes carry
The scent of new-mown hay.

BRANCHES

In the summer weather,
When gentle breezes blow,
This is how the branches sway,
Softly to and fro.
In the wintry weather,
When the cold winds blow,
This is how the branches move,
Tossing to and fro.

POPPY DANCE

Nod to the left and nod to the right,
    Whirl about, twirl about,
    Poppies so bright.

Bow to the left and bow to the right,
    Whirl about, twirl about,
    Red, pink and white.

Bend to the left and bend to the right,
    Whirl about, twirl about,
    Dance with delight.

Sway to the left and sway to the right,
    Whirl about, twirl about,
    Curtsey: Goodnight!

DANCE OF THE POPPY

See the ballet dancer
    In her scarlet gown,
Pirouetting on her toes,
    Light as thistledown.

See her lovely curtsey
    As the breeze blows by,
Spreading wide her petals
    Like a butterfly.

See the ballet dancer
  Swaying in the sun;
When the day is ended,
  Poppy's dance is done.

VERSE 1 Children dance on tip-toe on the spot.

VERSE 2 Children make graceful curtseys, holding out skirts to suggest the petals.

VERSE 3 Lines 9 and 10 Children sway trunks, head arms and hands.

Lines 11 and 12 Children become limp and relax to the floor.

TREES

Today we'll be all kinds of trees
Gently swaying in the breeze;
First a poplar, tall and straight,
Slowly moving by the gate.
Now a willow, small and lank,
Hanging o'er the river bank.

Although the wood is cold and bare
A large, broad oak is standing there.
Here a tiny mouse I see,
Curled up small beneath the tree
Like a tiny, rounded ball.
He doesn't seem to move at all.

THE CHESTNUT TREES

We are lovely chestnut trees,
Leaves all shaking in the breeze.
See us stand so straight and high,
Looking upwards to the sky.
Wave our branches so—and so—
Then make shade for flowers below.

Children stand in a single line, or in a double line to form an "avenue".

LINES 1 AND 2 Finger movements.

LINES 3 AND 4 Faces turned upwards.

LINES 5 AND 6 Arms waved to left and to right, then spread out.

THE PUSSY-WILLOW

The pussy-willow's bloom is soft,
    Soft as my pussy's paws,
And pussy-willows do not scratch,
    They have not any claws.

We gather branches in the spring,
    And see the shining gold
Of little paws along the stem—
    So furry-like to hold!

VERSE 1 Children make gentle, stroking movements with their hands.

VERSE 2 Children stretch upward to pick branches and then again gently touch the bloom.

THE WILLOWS

In winter the willows are gaunt and bare,
Standing so forlornly there.
But spring soon comes and the slender leaves
Flutter gaily in the breeze.
They bathe their tips in the stream that passes,
Flowing gently through waving grasses.

LABURNUM

The Lady Laburnum,
Elegant, tall,
Gracefully stands near
The garden wall.

Her long golden tresses
Are combed by the breeze,
An adornment to fit
A queen among trees.

The Lady Laburnum,
Stately but sweet,
Brings sunlit joy
To a dull city street.

ON THE BRIDGE

I love to idle by the bridge
And watch the lazy stream
Go flowing calmly underneath,
Clear in the sunlight's gleam,
The minnows darting to and fro
And the weeds that gently sway.
I could spend hours just gazing down
On a warm summer's day!

THE STREAM

From the lonely moor where the curlews cry,
And the bracken fronds wave green and high,
A little stream comes dancing down,
Her sun-warmed waters peaty-brown,
Over the boulders leaping, dashing,
On rounded pebbles tumbling, splashing.

Past heathery knolls and clambering sheep
She races down the hillside steep,
Then, weary, sinks to the woodland cool,
To rest at last in a tree-fringed pool,
Where dreaming alders, bending low,
Watch in her depths the sunset's glow.

SECTION III

ANIMALS: BEASTS, INSECTS AND BIRDS

LITTLE SQUIRREL

Little squirrel's fast asleep,
He's slept all winter through.
He's slept through cold and frosty nights,
And in the daytime too.

Little squirrel starts to wake,
Spring is here at last.
He shakes himself and looks around,
Yes, winter days are past.

Little squirrel wants some food,
He searches for his store.
He gobbles those nuts quickly up,
Then hunts about for more.

Little squirrel runs about,
And leaps from tree to tree.
He thinks of summer days ahead
And rubs his paws with glee.

Little squirrel's feeling tired.
Now stars begin to peep.
He slowly curls up in his nest
And soon he's sound asleep.

THE SQUIRREL

The squirrel awakes from his short, cosy sleep,
And slowly uncurls from his head to his feet.
He scratches his head and peeps from his tree,
And wonders where sweet, tasty acorns may be.

He climbs from his nest to a bough of the tree
And down on the grass lots of nuts he can see.
He quietly springs to the food on the ground—
So swiftly he jumps that he makes not a sound.

He picks up a nut in his two tiny paws,
He bites with his teeth and nibbles and gnaws.
Feeling thirsty, he drinks from a river near by
Then climbs a tall tree reaching right to the sky.

Now he washes his whiskers, his ears and his face,
For he's ready to run and to jump and to chase.
Then he springs to a branch of a tall tree near by
And watches the birds flying high in the sky.

MR. TORTOISE

Someone is stirring in his nest of hay,
Someone pushes soft soil and dead leaves away;
Up into the sunshine comes a little nose,
Off into the garden Mr. Tortoise goes.

His hard shell is heavy, he can only creep,
All through the winter he has lain asleep,
Waiting for the sunshine to send the snow away
And let him take a walk on a fine spring day.

LINES I AND 2 Children gradually stir and make gentle, firm,
"pushing" movements with heads and trunks.

LINES 3 AND 4 Children begin slow, heavy movement which
continues in second verse.

WHO GOES THERE?

Somebody slept through the frost and the snow,
All curled up with nose to toe.
Somebody woke and crept out of bed,—
He sniffed around and poked out his head.
Somebody felt a warm ray of sun:
"Splendid!" he grunted. "Cold winter is done."
Beetles and insects and slugs beware,
Hedgehog so hungry is taking the air!

THE MOLE

All winter long he slept on the moor,
But now he slowly opens his door,
He pushes and digs, until at last
He sees that winter has really passed.
He sniffs and wriggles his tiny nose.
Oh surely now, not another doze!
Ah no, he's creeping out of his hole
He's small and dark—a velvet mole.

The sleepy mole is now emerging
Happy to know the plants are growing,
The trees are in bud, the sky is blue
Oh there is so much for a mole to do!
Everyone's busy, new life has won,
And mole creeps on to find all the fun,
Squirrel, the rabbit and mouse are near,
Now they are sure that spring is here.

THE DORMOUSE

All winter through the dormouse sleeps
Curled up in his hole so warm and deep.
He raises his head and sniffs the air
To see if his friends are safe elsewhere.

No sign of danger, so now uncurled
He creeps outside to view the world.
The flowers are out, he gleefully sees,
And tiny buds have burst on the trees.

Shyly he strolls about the wood
His nose to the ground, oh it smells so good!
He looks up at the sky so blue and white
And down at the ground so green and bright.

When he's eaten his store of acorns and nuts
It's back to his hole over hillocks and ruts,
Then he curls up small and closes his eyes,
In his nest so cosy he quietly lies.

A TADPOLE GAME

Little wriggling tadpoles,
In and out the reeds,
Darting, rippling to and fro,
Nibbling at the weeds.

Silently across the pond
Now glides Mrs. Duck.
Little tadpoles quickly turn,
When they hear her cluck!

CATERPILLARS

When summer is over and autumn leaves fall,
Big and fat caterpillars creep on the wall.

They turn round their heads until they have spied
Some holes in the wall in which they can hide.

Now into their bedrooms they silently creep;
Each wraps itself into a blanket to sleep.

And there they lie still the long Winter through;
They seem to be dead—but this is not true.

For when Summer returns each wriggles about,
Tears down its blanket and then scrambles out.

See! Over their heads are wings folded high,
For each grub has changed to a gay butterfly!

They spread out their wings to air in the sun,
Then think that to try them would surely be fun!

So they fold—and then spread them—fold—and then spread,
Oh! beautiful wings, blue, yellow and red.

Then, when they are ready and eager to fly,
Away they all flutter to flowers near by.

They are hungry and thirsty and, sure, it is bliss
To sip the sweet nectar from that flower and this!

When breakfast is over they all fly away
To play in the sunshine and make the world gay.

The children act as the teacher reads the lines slowly.

VERSE 1 Children representing caterpillars, creep slowly.

VERSE 2 Turn heads this way and that, caterpillar-fashion.

VERSE 3 Line 1 Change course a little. Line 2 Roll over two or three times. Finish on back with legs and arms stretched and crossed stiffly to represent a chrysalis.

VERSE 4 Lie stiff and still.

VERSE 5 Line 1 Wriggle, still with legs and arms crossed. Line 2 Uncross legs and arms smartly and sit up.

VERSE 7 Line 1 Stretch out arms.

VERSE 8 Line 1 Fold "wings" above head, then spread them out alternately with the spoken words.

VERSE 9 Line 1 Stand with "wings" still extended. Line 2 Fly a short distance in any direction.

VERSE 10 "Butterflies" dart here and there in the limited space, settling on one flower and then another.

VERSE 11 Line 1 "Butterflies" fly right away, as far as they can go.

THE BUTTERFLY

Can you see the butterfly
With brightly coloured wing
Fluttering, fluttering, O so high
Amongst the birds that sing?

It lightly settles on a flower,
Its wings it folds up tight,
Then it's on its way again
And flutters out of sight.

This could suggest movement for hands only.

LINES 1 TO 4 Children flutter hands over their heads, moving them to and fro.

LINES 5 AND 6 Children gently fold hands.

LINES 7 AND 8 Children resume fluttering movements.
Alternatively the children may themselves be the butterflies.

BUTTERFLIES

Dancing, fluttering
Carelessly by
Under the gleaming
Summer sky,
They haunt the grasses,
Light as air,
Rising here
And dipping there.

Meadow Brown,
Red Admiral,
Peacock and
Bright Tortoiseshell—
All so splendid
As they dance by
Under the sunlit
Summer sky!

THE HUMBLE-BEE

Rumble, tumble,
Humble-bee!
Through the garden
Boomingly,
While the summer sun
Beats down
On your coat
Of golden-brown.

All day long
You come and go,
Where the shining
Blossoms blow,
Sipping every sweet
You see,
Rumble, tumble,
Humble-bee!

THIRST

A long large crocodile lay basking in the sun,
The day was warm,
The sky was blue,
And he was having fun.
But the hot sand tickled him, and his throat was getting dry.
He stretched himself,
He smacked his jaws:
A pool had caught his eye.
The cooling water tempted him, he sidled to the bank,
The water gleamed,
Cold, crystal clear,
So there he stayed and drank.

THE LILY POND

Here the water-lilies rest
On the water's peaceful breast.

Here he dances, jewel-bright,
Dragon-fly in darting flight.

In the depths, clear, green and cold,
Lazy fish make streaks of gold.

Lilies, goldfish, dragon-fly,
Underneath a summer sky;

All so quiet that they seem
Lost within a summer dream.

MR. FOX

Only the brook was singing,
And one clear nightingale,
When down the hedge at twilight
Went Mr. Fox, Mr. Fox,
Dragging his bushy tail.

Softly, softly walking
Where silver puffballs float
Beside the wild-rose hedges
Went Mr. Fox, Mr. Fox,
In chestnut-coloured coat.

He stopped and looked and listened,
As still as any stone;
Then whisk!—into the woodlands
Went Mr. Fox, Mr. Fox,
And left me there alone.

LIONS AND TIGERS

The lion roars, the tiger growls,
Their mouths are open wide,
Then, suddenly, they snap them closed,
To trap their prey inside.
They chew their food with strong, white teeth
Which sparkle when they smile,
They lick their lips with long pink tongues
Then yawn, and sleep awhile.

Children may make their hands imitate the movements of the
animals described.

GOING TO THE ZOO

When we have a holiday
Oh, what shall we do?
We'll take a little bus ride
And go to the zoo.

We like the monkeys best of all,
We like the way they jump.
They climb up high with hands and feet,
And sometimes slide down bump!

The elephant is big and strong,
Just watch what he can do.
He'll take a penny in his trunk
And ring a bell for you.

The giraffe has such a long, long neck,
He stretches up so high
To reach the top leaves on the tree.
He seems to touch the sky.

The sea-lions lie beside their pool,
They look around to see
The keeper coming with the fish
He brings them for their tea.

The kangaroos stand very still,
Just looking all around,
Then suddenly away they go,
All leaping off the ground.

THE UNHAPPY DONKEY

A sturdy little donkey
dressed in sober grey,
Took into his long-eared head
that he would run away.

So when a little open
he saw the stable door,
He ran as if he never would
come back there any more.

Away the donkey galloped,
through the open door,
And ran and ran and ran and ran,
till he could run no more.

A GALLOPING RHYME

I had a white charger,
Most splendid and bold:
His hoofs were like silver,
His mane was of gold,
He stamped his bright hoofs,
And he tossed up his mane
And he galloped away to the castles of Spain.

Wild horses come galloping over the plains.
They toss their proud heads
And shake their long manes;
They fly through the forest,
Jump over the streams,
Race over the hill-tops,
Are lost in my dreams.

CAT

I have a pet, he's fluffy and white,
His eyes are green, they shine at night,
His fur is thick, and warm, and deep,
His whiskers waggle when he's asleep.

His tail is long with a kink at the end,
But his claws are sharp and my skin can rend,
He laps his milk with a tongue so rough,
Then he sits and purrs as he cleans his fluff.

THE CAT

When the cat uncurls her paws
She stretches out her long sharp claws
And slowly moves them to and fro,
Sometimes high and sometimes low.
Then she brings her claws up tight
And shakes her paws with all her might.

A CAT'S DAY

I have a little cat,
She's black and white and grey.
She sits before the fire
And dreams the day away.

At noon she stirs herself
And stands and stretches long.
And then she purrs to me
A pleasant little song.

I know just what she wants:
A plate of golden cream,
And when she's had her fill
She licks her whiskers clean.

She'll stroll about the house,
At everything she'll peep.
Then if she's quite content
She'll curl up fast asleep.

MY CAT

I have a big, black pussy cat,
And Sooty is her name,
And every time my bedtime comes
She loves to have a game.

One day, she found a ball of wool
And got herself entangled;
She even had it round her ears
And on her tail it dangled.

She looked so funny moving round,
But mummy had to stop her;
For this bright wool that she had there
Was part of my new jumper.

DICKORY DOCK

Dickory Dock was a little grey mouse,
He ran here and there all over the house,
He ran on the mat, and he jumped on the chair—
In fact, he ran about everywhere,
He was up on the clock when it chimed out One
And didn't that Dickory Run—Run—Run.

BREAKFAST FOR THE BIRDS

The birds are awake so early each day,
And all look so busy with no time to play.
They are searching for breakfast so I have been told,
But I don't think that I'd like to eat in the cold.

The birds seem so happy and don't seem to mind,
They are pleased with each insect and worm they can find.
I know if I helped them they'd just fly away,
So I sit in the warm house to watch them each day.

BIRDS OF A FEATHER

Birds that swoop and dip to fly,
Soaring higher in the sky,
Sparrows small, but brown and bright,
Swallows sailing high in flight,
Birds of feather, big and small,
With fluttering wings and merry call.

Birds in cages who jump and hop,
Climbing, twisting to the top,
Birds on perches gaily swinging,
Busy thrushes always singing,
Flying alone, in pairs together,
Martins, finches, birds of a feather.

SWIFTS

To and fro
And round about,
Darting in the eaves
And out,
Go the swifts
In joyous flight
In the evening's
Lingering light.

After the hot
Summer's day,
Now it's cool
They're out to play,
Screaming, whirling
Overhead
Till the last
Gold light has fled!

FLUFFY YELLOW CHICKS

Ten fluffy yellow chicks
Pecking here and there,
Ten fluffy yellow chicks
Running everywhere,
Ten fluffy yellow chicks
Tired of having fun,
Ten fluffy yellow chicks
Sleeping in the sun.

QUACK-QUACK

Two little ducks went out to play,
    Quack-quack, Quack-quack.
Over the hills and far away,
    Quack-quack, Quack-quack.

"I wish that we could always stay,"
    Quack-quack, Quack-quack.
"For it is such a lovely day,"
    Quack-quack, Quack-quack.

They had so much delightful play,
    Quack-quack, Quack-quack.
"Let's go there again," they say,
    Quack-quack, Quack-quack.

For the chorus lines the children make each hand into a "duck's head" and move fingers and thumb rhythmically. This is a useful movement for younger children who have not yet full control of separate fingers.

WILD GEESE

Over grey seas
The wild geese come,
Wild birds seeking
A winter home.

They fly all night,
Close to the sky,
Calling to the stars
Their strange, wild cry.

Where the cold tide creeps
In lines of foam,
To wild, windy marshes
The wild geese come.

MR. CROW AND MR. ROOK

Over the field soft-furred with snow,
Into the sunset flapping low,
Home by himself goes Mr. Crow.

Over the elms beside the brook,
High in the cold blue evening—look!
Home with his friends goes Mr. Rook.

ROBIN'S SONG

Robin hops and Robin stops,
Robin cocks his head;
Robin flaps his wings and sings
Waiting to be fed.

Robin hops and Robin stops,
Robin nods his head;
Robin flaps his wings and sings:
"Thank you for my bread."

Then he pipes, perched on a tree,
"Don't forget a drink for me,
Tra-la-la and tra-la-lee,
Merry Robin will I be."

SILENT WINGS

Who sails by on silent wings,
Round of head and round of eye?—
Strange and ghostly he goes by.

Who sails by on silent wings,
Curved of beak and quick of ear?—
Softly, softly he draws near.

Who sails by on silent wings?
Owl the Hunter, sharp of eye;
He it is goes gliding by.

DORMOUSE

"Now winter is coming,"
The Dormouse said,
"I must be thinking
Of going to bed."
So he curled himself up
As small as he could,
And went fast asleep
As a dormouse should.

Children curl up and go to sleep like the Dormouse.

LITTLE SQUIRREL

When the golden leaves are falling
On an autumn day,
Little squirrel in the forest
Has no time for play.

Hurry, scurry! Where the branches
Cluster thick and low,
Little squirrel, never pausing,
Scampers to and fro.

Nuts she gathers from the bushes
For her winter store—
Little squirrel won't be hungry
When the wild winds roar.

AUTUMN

"The leaves are brown," the robin sang,
"And winter days are near.
What shall we do in the woods and fields
When frost and snow are here?"

"I'll go to sleep," the squirrel said,
"Inside my cosy tree.
Just now I'm storing nuts away
In case I wake, you see."

"A good idea," the hedgehog called,
"I too will sleep and rest;
Beneath the hedge, with leaves and grass,
I've made a lovely nest."

"The pond's my home," said little frog,
"So that's where I shall go.
I'll never feel the snow and ice
Down in the mud below."

"I'll stay awake," red robin sang,
And fluffed his feathers gay.
"I'll sing a merry cheerful song
On the coldest winter day."

When night comes down on the children's eyes
And all in the house is still,
For busy folk it is time to rise
In the Wood Land over the hill.
There are those who wake when the moon is high;
They have slept for the whole long day.
With a silent shake or a call or cry,
They are off on the trail away.
The Owl, who hides from the sunlight's beam,
Hark!—there is his "Too-hoo-hoo!"
The Vole who lives by the gurgling stream
Steals out in the darkness too.
The Stoat, the Rat,
And the squeaking Bat
All open their keen little eyes
And rise.
And the Hedgehog peeps from his cosy nest
And hurries out with the rest.
The bark of the Fox shows he's astir,
And the Rabbit shivers within his fur,
And the sleepy Dormouse wakes at last—
There's none in the wood can move so fast.
Each one on his trail is off away
And never comes back till the dawn of day.

SECTION IV

THINGS TO DO

LIFT YOUR ARMS

Lift your arms, lift your arms,
Lift them very high.
Stretch your arms, stretch your arms,
Right into the sky.

Now drop your arms, drop your arms,
Drop them to your knees,
And swing your arms, swing your arms,
As gently as you please.

UP AND DOWN

Nod your head,
Bend your knees,
Grow as tall as Christmas trees.

On your knees
Slowly fall,
Curl yourself into a ball.

Raise your head,
Jump up high,
Wave your hand and say "Goodbye".

LOUD AND SOFT

Clap, clap, clap, clap,
Clap your hands and twist them round.
Tap, tap, tap, tap,
Tap them gently on the ground.

Stamp, stamp, stamp, stamp,
Stamp your feet with all your might.
Tap, tap, tap, tap,
Tap your toes so soft and light.

Rock, rock, rock, rock,
Now it's time to go to bed.
Hush, hush, hush, hush,
Shut your eyes, you sleepy head.

HOP A LITTLE

Hop a little, jump a little,
One, two, three.
Run a little, skip a little,
Tap one knee.
Bend a little, stretch a little,
Nod your head.
Yawn a little, sleep a little
In your bed.

I stamp my feet
   And wriggle my toes
And clap my hands
   As the music goes.

I reach to the sky
   And touch the ground,
Up and down to the
   Music sound.

I rock to and fro
   The way the wind blows;
It's fun to go
   Where the music goes.

SKIPPING

Over my head and under my toes,
Watch the way my skipping rope goes.
Over my head, ten toes off the ground,
See my rope swing round and round.
I can skip slowly, I can skip fast;
Watch my rope go whirling past.
Over my head and under my toes,
It's fun the way my skipping rope goes.

Feather so light,
  Up in the air,
Floating and flying
  Everywhere.
A gentle puff
  From a tiny breeze
And off you go
  Just as you please
Fluttering and gliding
  All around,
Then falling gently
  To the ground.

FLYING

Skipping, skipping,—
  Never tripping,
Lightly on my feet.

Hopping, hopping,—
  Never stopping,
Up and down the street.

Creeping, creeping;
  Baby's sleeping,
Do not make him cry.

Flying, flying,
  See me trying,
Trying to reach the sky.

Lightly, lightly,
Snowflakes flying,
Swirling, whirling,
Softly lying,
Snowflakes lying . . .

Quickly, quickly,
Swallows darting,
This way, that way,
Meeting, parting,
Swallows darting . . .

Slowly, sadly,
Old men going,
Walking, talking,
To-and-fro-ing,
Old men going . . .

Ponies, ponies,
Tossing manes,
Stamping, tramping
Over the plains,
Tossing manes . . .

Tails a-twitching,
Small mice frisking,
Never touching
Twisting, whisking,
Small mice frisking.

TICKY-TOUCH-WOOD

Tick-ticky-touch-wood!—Run for your life,
Or Ticky will get you before you say knife!
Quick—to the apple tree—now to the gate—
Now to the railings, before it's too late;
Run like a greyhound, or run like a hare,
Touch the wood quickly, before he gets there;
Hear him behind you—he's as close as can be—
Ah, Ticky-touch-wood you cannot touch me.

DAILY DOZEN

On Monday I will leap up high,
Then stand and stretch up to the sky.
On Tuesday I will crouch down low,
Then like a flower slowly grow
Until, on Wednesday, I'm so tall
That I can climb onto the wall.
On Thursday I will skip around,
Then slowly curl up on the ground.
On Friday I will bend my knees,
Then gallop off among the trees.
On Saturday I'm going to hop,
Then spin around just like a top.
On Sunday, I will nod my head—
And then it's time to go to bed.

CLOSE YOUR FINGERS

Close your fingers,
Open them wide,
Make a nest and peep inside.

Open your fingers,
Make them clap,
Lay your hands low in your lap.

Flutter your fingers
To the sky;
Give them wings like birds that fly.

Dance your fingers
Round and round—
Autumn leaves fall to the ground.

Open your fingers
Through them peep,
Fold them now, sing them to sleep.

TREAD WITH ME

Softly, softly tread with me
Down the winding stair,
The house is still, all fast asleep,
So softly tread with care.

A noise is heard, a screeching sound,
Listen, what can it be?
'Tis only an owl on nightly prowl,
So softly tread with me.

Softly, softly tread with me,
Up the winding stair,
Back to bed, so safe and sound,
Softly tread with care.

SECTION V

BUSY DAYS

LAZY-BONES

He lay there snugly curled up tight
Between the warm sheets milky-white,
Oh so cosy! What a shame
That Mummy soon would call his name.

He slowly stretched each tiny toe
And slid his feet far down below,
Until he couldn't feel again
The warm, soft spot where he had lain.

Then he poked his pinky nose
Above the cuddly, friendly clothes,
And felt the smart of icy air
Which sent strange tingles through his hair.

Bravely though, he didn't stop,
But pulled both hands up to the top.
He stretched and stretched with all his might
Until he felt quite stiff and tight.

At last he went quite limp and slack
And then he pushed the covers back—
—Washed and dressed by Mummy's call,
Good, he's early after all!

This poem offers opportunity for supported stretching movements.
The children lie on the floor and pretend to be in bed.

WAKING UP

I wake in the morning and stretch my arms wide,
Over my head and down to my side;
Reach up for my dressing gown high on the door,
And stoop for my slippers that lie on the floor.
Oh dear! One has fallen far under the bed,
I can just about reach it—Ouch! that was my head.
When I've had a good wash, brushed my teeth and my hair,
I creep from my room, put one foot on the stair
And softly descend, to where Mummy below
Is making the breakfast. I call out "Peep-bo",
Then give her a hug and sit down on my stool,
Say my grace, eat breakfast and run off to school.

This poem offers opportunity for stretching both high and low, as well as for carrying out a sequence of actions.

POLISHING

The highest shelf is very high.
The lowest one is very low.
To polish them all will take some time
So shake out the duster,
You mustn't be slow.
Stretch to the top shelf, higher now.
Polish it well until it shines.
Now bend to the lowest, crouch right down,
And polish it well for the very last time.

SWEEPING

Pick up the broom to sweep the floor,
Sweep the dust carefully out of the door.
Remember the corners and under the mat
And mind where you step as you sweep past the cat.
Carefully now, sweep the dust to a pile,
Now you can sit and rest for a while.

BRUSHES

There's a brush for sweeping the kitchen,
And a brush for sweeping the stairs;
There's a brush for scrubbing the front doorstep,
And a brush for brushing best chairs.

There's a brush for swishing the bath out,
And a brush for cleaning my nails;
There's a brush for teeth: mine's a blue one,
And a brush that stays beside pails.

There's a brush to keep in my paint box,
And a brush for brushing my hair;
There's a brush for clothes on the hat-stand,
And a brush marked PET by pup's chair.

There's a brush that's used by the roadman,
And a brush that's like a stiff mop;
It goes all the way up our chimney,
Right to the very top.

GLUE

My hands are all sticky
   They've been in the glue,
I'll lift them up slowly
   And show them to you.
They've now stuck together.
   I'll pull them apart,
Then put them in water
   Oh dear, how they smart!

CLEANING OUR HANDS

On your fingers there are raindrops,
   Shake them off! Shake them off!
On your left one, now your right one,
   Shake them off! Shake them off!

Look! Your hands are very muddy.
   Clean them well! Clean them well!
And your arms are very dirty,
   Clean them well! Clean them well!

Now your hands they should be soapy,
   Rub them hard! Rub them hard!
Down your thumbs and round your fingers,
   Rub them hard! Rub them hard!

Dry your hands now they are cleaner,
   Up and down! Up and down!
Show them me. Ah! That is better,
   Up and down! Up and down!

BUSY DAYS

Monday is our washing day,
    And if the weather's fine
I wash and rinse my dolly's clothes
    And hang them on the line.

On baking day they let me start
    With board and rolling pin;
I make a tasty apple tart
    With lots of sugar in.

And now I'll tell another thing
    I'm sure you'd like to know;
I have a bright new thimble,
    And I'm learning how to sew.

VERSE 1 Children make washing and rinsing movements with
their hands.
VERSE 2 Children make "rolling" and shaping movements with
their hands.
VERSE 3 Children imitate sewing action.

SPRING CLEANING

Shake the mats, shake the mats, shake the mats, do!
Bang them and beat them and make them like new;

Rub-a-dub—rub-a-dub—rub-a-dub go,
Wash all the curtains and hang them to blow!

Sweep the floors, sweep the floors, sweep the floors clean—
Here is a doll's house that's fit for a Queen!

MY WASHING DAY

Today I shall be busy;
I hope it will keep fine,
As I shall have some washing
To hang out on the line.

My family of dollies
Do have such grubby clothes.
But how they get so dirty,
Well, no one ever knows.

I'll wash and rinse and shake them,
And, after this is done,
My family will help me
To hang them in the sun.

When all are dry and folded,
I guess my work is done.
But don't you think that washing
Is really rather fun?

WASHING DAY

Washing day, washing day.
Mother *rubs* the clothes this way.
Rub-a-dub, rub-a-dub,
Up and down inside the tub.

Washing day, washing day.
Mother *wrings* the clothes this way.
Turn and turn and turn about,
Wringing all the water out.

Washing day, washing day.
Mother *hangs* the clothes this way.
Pegs them up upon the line.
Then the sun begins to shine.

Washing day, washing day.
Mother *irons* the clothes this way
Left and right, left and right,
All so smooth and snowy white.

Washing day, washing day,
Busy, busy washing day.

LET'S BAKE A CAKE!

Stir butter with sugar
   Until it looks white;
Add eggs one by one—
   Beat them fluffy and light.
Mix flower, spice and currants,
   Then set all to bake,
And soon, when it's tea-time,
   We'll taste our new cake.

Put the bowl upon the table,
Stir as smoothly as you're able.
Stir and wish, and stir and wish.
That is what you have to do,
To make your Christmas wish come true.

Stir the sugar, flour and fruit,
Silver charms so small and cute.
Stir and wish, and stir and wish.
Softly to myself I say,
"I hope it snows on Christmas Day."

MY GARDEN

I can't come out to play today,
I've far too much to do,
I'm digging in my garden
And sowing seeds there too.
I'm raking and I'm hoeing,
And I'm pulling up the weeds;
I'm picking stones and pebbles
Which might upset my seeds.

I'm searching very carefully
For slugs and snails and such,
To tell them, quite politely,
My plants *they must not touch.*
Then, when I've finished gardening,
I'll put my tools away,
And tell the man who lives next door
About my busy day.

AT THE GARAGE

Tap, tap-tap, tap, tap,
We'll mend your car for you.
Tap, tap-tap, tap, tap,
We've lots of work to do.

We'll pump the tyres up full of air,
Oh, there are four to do,
Two at the front, two at the back—
Now that job's done for you.

Please put some petrol in the tank,
One gallon, two, three, four,
And screw the cap on very tight,
Don't spill any on the floor.

Oh will the engine start up now?
Let's turn the handle round.
Br-rr-rr-rr, yes, off she goes
Now here's your bill—one pound!

HOME TIME

Time to pack our bricks up,
Listen for the bell.
Then we put our coats on,
Hats and gloves as well.
Skip home to our mothers
Through the garden gate.
Sit down to our tea now,
Cream cakes on the plate!

A VERSE ABOUT ME

I'm scrubbing my teeth,
Scrub, scrub.
I'm washing my hands,
Rub, rub.
I'm brushing my hair,
Brush, brush.
I'm climbing upstairs,
Hush, hush.
I'm going to bed,
Creep, creep.
I'm in bed . . .
   yawn,
      yawn,
         yawn,
           asleep.

SECTION VI

PEOPLE

SKIPPING SUSAN

Little Susan learnt to skip—
   Skip, skip—skip, skip, skip,
Round and round her rope did slip—
   Skip, skip—skip, skip, skip.

Little Susan learnt to hop—
   Hop, hop—hop, hop, hop,
We thought that she would never stop—
   Hop, hop—hop, hop, hop.

Little Susan stretched up tall—
   Tall, tall—tall, tall, tall,
Then she made herself so small—
   Small, small—small, small, small.

Little Susan goes to sleep—
   Sleep, sleep, softly sleep,
As the stars begin to peep—
   Sleep, sleep, softly sleep.

JENNY

Jenny, Jenny, sweep the leaves,
Sweep them in a pile,
Jenny, Jenny brush the leaves,
And then just rest awhile.

Daddy, Daddy burn the leaves,
Burn them all at once.
Jenny, Jenny watch the leaves,
As merrily they dance.

Jenny, Jenny climb the stairs,
Climb them one by one,
You have had a busy day,
But now your work is done.

THE LOST KITTEN

JOHN:
Jennifer Jane, Jennifer Jane,
Why are you crying outside in the rain?

JENNIFER JANE:
I can't find my kitten; he slipped through the door.

JOHN:
I'll help you to find him; don't cry any more.
Shall we look over here? Now we'll look over there.
Is that your wee kitten?

JENNIFER JANE:
It is I declare!

WHERE IS SHE?

TEACHER:
They looked through the farmhouse,
And called down the lane,
But there wasn't a sign of Elizabeth Jane.

CHORUS OF CHILDREN (*Searching*):
Elizabeth Jane! Elizabeth Jane!
Where have you gone, Elizabeth Jane?

TEACHER:
They ran to the orchard
And called her in vain:
There wasn't a sound from Elizabeth Jane.

CHORUS, *as before*

TEACHER:
They went to the hayfield
And tried once again:
And there in the hay slept Elizabeth Jane.

CHORUS:
Elizabeth Jane! Elizabeth Jane!
So here's where you're hiding, Elizabeth Jane!

ELIZABETH JANE:
You've wakened me up from a beautiful dream!
I was just sitting down to some strawberries and cream.

CHORUS:
Go back to sleep then, and dream it again
                    (*She lies down*)
We won't spoil the feast for Elizabeth Jane!
                    (*They tiptoe away*)

PLAYTIME

I'm a little boy,
    I've got a spinning top;
I can make it hum,
    And I can make it hop.

I'm a little girl,
    I've got a Teddy Bear;
I cuddle him all day,
    I take him everywhere.

I'm a little boy,
    I've got a lovely kite;
I fly it very high,
    And nearly out of sight.

I'm a little girl,
    I've got a ball—so new;
Will you play with me?
    I'd like to play with you!

CREEPING JENNY

Poor old Jenny,
Beset with care,
Has laid her money
She knows not where!
And all the village
Looks out and sees
Creeping Jenny
Upon her knees!

Over the grass
On hands and toes,
Wistful Jenny
A-weeping goes.
"Foolish me,
To forget!" she cries,
And she peers round her
With her anxious eyes,
All for money
So lately earned,
And leaving never
A stone unturned!
And then at last
She delights to trace
Her unspent wealth
In a secret place,
And finds, or ever
The tale be told,
Her hoard of pence
Is a heap of gold!

This verse could be spoken while children mime the action of "Creeping Jenny", who finds at last her golden flowers.

N.B. The leaves of creeping Jenny grow in pairs like two round pennies, so people once called it Herb twopence. It is a little plant that trails close to the ground so it was also called Wandering Jenny! Because of the bright gold of its flowers it was given the name "String of Sovereigns".

Many people grow Creeping Jenny in their gardens. First come the green-penny leaves, then the flowers like golden money.

THE BAKER

I like the jolly baker
Who brings me my bread,
He has a rosy, smiling face,
A white cap on his head,
He opens up his basket
And Mother bends to see—
Bread rolls, brown bread,
What shall we have for tea?

And, yes, he has some doughnuts!
They're sugary and round,
He has jam tarts and crumpets, too,
And what is this I've found?
A man made out of ginger,
He's brought it just for me.
I'll hurry in and eat it.
It's time now for my tea.

POSTMAN BOLD

Look at me, a postman bold,
Walking through the wet and cold.

Rat-a-tat. Rat-a-tat.
Walking through the wet and cold.

Up and down the street I go,
On my hands I blow and blow.

Rat-a-tat. Rat-a-tat.
On my hands I blow and blow.

Here's a letter. Rat, tat, tat.
Now it's fallen on the mat.

Rat-a-tat. Rat-a-tat.
Now it's fallen on the mat.

I have quite a heavy sack,
Which I carry on my back.

Rat-a-tat. Rat-a-tat.
Which I carry on my back.

THE POSTMAN

Ratterty tatterty tatterty tat.
How many letters will fall on the mat?
Brown ones for Daddy—pink ones for Pat,
A postcard for Mummy from Uncle Nat.
Ratterty tatterty tatterty tat,
How many for me will fall on the mat?

TRADESMEN

Knock, knock, knock; who goes there?
Is it the postman with the snowy white hair?
Knock, knock, knock; who was that?
Was it the coalman with his bulging sack?
Knock, knock, knock; who's at the door?
Is it the milkman with bottles galore?
Knock, knock, knock; who can that be?
Perhaps it's Daddy come home for tea.

THE RAG AND BONE MAN

Here comes the rag and bone man
With his pony and his cart,
His face is red and shiny,
And he isn't very smart.
He wears a pair of trousers
That are baggy at the knees,
His handkerchief is spotted
And it flutters in the breeze.
He shouts so loud and hoarsely
As he drives along the street,
He is the oddest fellow
You could ever wish to meet.

THIS IS THE WAY

This is the way the painter works,
    Sweeping his brushes to and fro.
This is the way the cobbler works,
    Tapping his nails all in a row.
This is the way the farmer works,
    Sowing corn in his fields to grow.
This is the way the baker works,
    Kneading and rolling his spongy dough.

ROUNDABOUT HORSES

The Roundabout Horses
Have come to the town;
To the sound of music
They ride up and down;
I never saw horses
As splendid as they
With their saddles of scarlet
And bridles so gay.

The Roundabout's roof
Is a wonderful sight,
All painted with colours
To give you delight;
With primrose and orange,
With blue and with red;
No wonder each horse
Tosses up his proud head!

The Roundabout's Horses
Are splendid and bold;
They jingle their bridles
Of silver and gold,
To the sound of the music
They go with a swing—
I am sure that each one
Is the steed of a king!

PLAYING AT CIRCUSES

I'm a little pony,
Trotting round the ring;
I paw the ground, and shake my head
To make my bright bells ding.

Now I am an elephant,
My steps are big and slow.
I swing my trunk and nod my head
Slowly to and fro.

Look at me, a laughing clown,
And see the tricks I do;
I clap my hands above my head
And bend my long legs too.

But now I feel so very tired
That I must sit awhile.
I fold my arms and keep quite still
And smile a happy smile.

THE BAND PASSES

One, two, one two one,
Bang! Bang! Beat that drum.
Clash! Clash! the cymbals go,
Beat them high, beat them low.

The Band is marching through the town,
See them pacing up and down,
Doors and windows open wide,
People peer from every side.

One, two, one two one,
Bang! Bang! Beat that drum,
Clash! Clash! the cymbals go,
Beat them high, beat them low.

Now they've passed along the street,
Quieter now the stamp of feet,
Into the distance goes the drum,
As windows close up one by one.

THE BAND

Have you ever heard a drummer
Beat a rhythm on his drum?
If you listen very closely,
I will show you how its done.

Have you ever heard the cymbals
When they're crashing out the beat?
If you haven't any cymbals,
Tap the rhythm with your feet.

Have you ever heard such music
Playing fast or slow,
While the trombones sing the tune out
And the trumpets loudly blow?

The children march to the rhythm and mime the actions of the
members of the band as they are mentioned.

MARCHING AT NIGHT

Left, right, left, right,
Soldiers marching by.
Left, right, left, right,
Spears towards the sky.
Left, right, left, right,
Gleaming armour bright.
Left, right, left, right,
Tramping through the night.

SECTION VII

PLAY, FANTASY AND MAGIC

TRAIN RIDE

Clickety-clack, clickety-clack,
The wheels fly over the railway track,
The fields slip past, the roads race by,
And cars seem to crawl as on we fly—
Diddle-de-do, diddle-de-do,
That's when over the points we go.
A station's coming! We're near a town!
The rhythm changes, the train slows down—
Diddle-de-dum, diddle-de-dum,
Out of the way, for here we come!
A screech of brakes, a puff of steam,
On to the platform the people stream.
A banging of doors and a shout, "Stand clear!"
The rattle of couplings soon we hear,
Then a puff and a jerk, and away we go,
Slowly at first, then *diddle-de-do*
Over the points, then *clickety-clack*
The wheels fly over the railway track.
Diddle-de-diddle-de-diddle-de-day—
A train roars by the other way,
A glimpse of a face, then we're flashing past
And nearing the end of our journey at last.
Familiar places we're passing again,
Looking quite different seen from the train.
The train pulls up with a jerk and a bump.
On to the platform, down we jump.
"Goodbye, Mr. Driver, we'll see you again.
We'll never forget our ride in your train,
With its *diddle-de-do* and the *clickety-clack*
As the wheels fly over the railway track."

TRAIN TALK

Clickety-clack! Clickety-clack,
Here comes the train along the track.
Chug-chug-choo, chug-chug-choo.
O, what a fuss and what a to-do!

Rickety-rack, rickety-rack
I can't stay here; I must get back.
Chuff-chuff-choo, chuff-chuff-choo:
Do hurry up; I can't wait for you!

With a wheeze and a sneeze
And a whistle and cough,
Slam go the doors and, hurray!
I'm off!

NOTE: Said in imitation of a train's rhythm.

THE SAND HEAP

In summer when the days are hot,
I have upon my garden plot
A heap of yellow sand for play—
I go there every Saturday.

I take my dolls, I take my bricks,
I take some shells and stones and sticks,
Some jars of water clean and cool,
A washing tub to make a pool.

I take some Plasticine, of course,
Some fir cones, tea things and my horse;
Some bottles, buckets, spades and tins,
And then at last the fun begins.

When I have settled down to play,
The lawn and flower beds fade away;
There is no garden any more,
And I am on a sandy shore.

I splash and paddle in the sea,
I make some sand pies for my tea,
I set my pirate ships a-float,
I build a castle, dig a moat.

I take a gallop on the sands,
I make a tunnel with my hands—
A railway line with bricks and stones,
A garden with my shells and cones.

And oh, how very hard it seems
To leave this country of my dreams,
The shining sea, the golden sands—
To brush my hair and wash my hands!

CEMENT MIXER

I'd like to be a mixer
Of cement, in a big fixer.
　David calls it "Top-o'-Tin"—
What is that?
Why, Tip-it-in:
Tip the stones
And grind them in
The big revolving
Iron bin.
　I want to grind and fix and mix
　And slap cement between the bricks—
　And round and round will go the bin—
But David calls it "Top-o'-Tin"!

WHO AM I?

The hat I wear has the widest brim,
The pony I ride is sleek and trim;
My spurs a-jingle as I gallop by—
Can you guess? Who am I?

With a red silk scarf around my head,
I pace the deck with an awful tread;
The "skull-and-cross" is the flag I fly,
For I'm the—well, who am I?

I raid the kitchen for chocolate cake,
Annoy everyone with the noises I make,
I'm into mischief—who can I be?
Did someone say, "It can't be me"?

SMOKE FAIRIES

A bonfire in our garden
Is burning bright today;
The flames, all red and golden,
Leap up like dancers gay,
And little, shy smoke fairies
Come stealing out to play.

Dressed in their wispy garments,
Out of the flames they fly,
Then gaily float and flutter
Above the treetops high,
Until they softly vanish
Into the gentle sky.

LINES 1 TO 4 With hands and arms children suggest the movements of the flames.
LINES 5 TO 12 Children dance lightly as the smoke fairies.

MAGIC

Twitching her tail, the witch's cat,
Lean and sleek, by the cauldron sat.
The fire burned bright and the wind blew cold,
And spells were strong in the days of old.

Now by the fire the black cats lie
And twitch their tails when the wind blows high.
Their green eyes dream of the dark night's ride
When they flew to the stars by the witches' side.

THE WITCH

Daughter of the moon, she rode by night
Silhouetted in the sky, an eerie sight.
She sat on her broom with her painted hat,
Her black flowing robes, and of course, her cat.
Her wizened face was crabbed and old,
Her chin was sharp, with a wart I'm told.
Deep set and evil, those were her eyes.
And when she cast spells they doubled in size.
Her nose was hooked and had nostrils wide,
Her mouth was a slit with large teeth inside.
Her fingers were thin, and bony, and strong.
Her nails were like talons and grotesquely long.
So beware, beware, for the moon is new,
Stay out of her path lest her curse falls on you.

THE WOOD WITCH*

The horny witch
Is in the wood.
Cross your fingers
And be good!
There she sits
Beneath the oak,
In her cap
And skinny cloak,
Making, mending,
While 'tis light,
Brooms for every
Fly-by-night.

* Wood Witch fungus or Stinkhorn

NIGHT ADVENTURE

All the house is quiet,
And everyone's in bed,
But when I try to go to sleep
Strange dreams come to my head.

Sometimes I dream of witches
Who live in woods so deep;
With large black cats and broomsticks
They move with stealthy creep.

I ride upon their broomsticks
And play with their black cats,
I make the fire and stir the pots
And wear their tall, dark hats.

When witches go to seek their prey,
We ride fast through the sky,
Off by night and back by dawn
So very high we fly.

I'm riding fast, up with the birds
Past the stars and moon.
I can see my home far off
So I'll be there quite soon.

Now I'm back, curled up in bed
And Mother's calling me.
I wash and dress and brush my hair
Before she counts to three.

Down in the wood where the bluebell grows,
There's a tiny copse where nobody goes,
For there in a cave, as deep as a well,
A warlock weaves a magic spell.

He wears a hat that is tall and black,
And a big, dark cloak flung over his back.
His face is old, and wrinkled, and sly,
With eyes of deep blue, like the summer sky.

His friends are the toads and spiders and rats.
He shares his den with seven black cats.
When the sun has gone and it is night,
He searches for herbs in the pale moonlight.

Then, through the night, when the world is asleep,
The herbs he will mix in his cauldron deep;
While all around the cats do stare—
Not a sound to be heard anywhere.

At the hour of twelve he leaves his home,
And in the wood till morning he'll roam.
What he does then, nobody knows,
For nobody walks where the warlock goes.

The sky is dark, the stars are bright,
The moon is shining too,
Inside a cave the witches meet
To mix their favourite brew.

They light a fire, and when it flames
They fetch a big black pot;
They fill it up with lizard's blood
Then wait until it's hot.

Each one has brought a magic charm
To put into the stew,
A spider's web, a fairy's wing,
A beetle's leg, or two.

They take a stick, and bending low
They stir the mixture round,
Then rub their fingers, old and cramped,
And stamp upon the ground.

Their wizened faces grin with glee
As round the pot they prance.
Their sharp eyes glisten in the dark,
Their cloaks swirl as they dance.

They drink, and then into the sky,
On broomsticks, swift and light,
They cackle hoarsely as they fly,
And soon are out of sight.

MOON FANTASY

Have you ever looked at the moon?
Sometimes he's got a face.
He moves around in his silvery shoon
Suspended up in space.

Sometimes he smiles at the children in bed
And watches them while they sleep.
Sometimes he has a big round head
As through the clouds he'll peep.

Tonight before you draw your curtain
Look up at the big white moon,
And you will see him, I am certain.
So goodnight children, sleep soon.

SAMSON FULLENGTH

He strode over houses and rivers and trees,
The tallest of towers only just reached his knees.
He held twenty people in only one hand
They all agreed afterwards: the view was just grand.
He ate thirteen bullocks at one midday meal,
At other meals too, he could eat a great deal.
He spoke, and our hats were blown from our heads,
He snored, and we trembled and shook in our beds.
He laughed and his mouth was open so wide
We could all scramble in and view the inside.
But in spite of his size, his voice and his strength,
He was gentle and kind—
      giant
       Samson Fullength.

GIANTS AND FAIRIES

Stamp, stamp, heavy and slow,
That is the way the giants go;
Thump, thump, clear the way,
Giants are going to town today.

Poppety, poppety, may we pass?
Fairies are dancing on the grass;
Trippety, trippety, here we go,
Dainty fairies on tip, tip-toe.

THE RAINBOW MEN

Each night when everyone's in bed
And everything is still,
The funniest little men appear
Upon the window sill.

They're very small and rather fat,
Their hair is long and red,
They wear short coats of navy blue
With saucepans on their heads.

Their shoes are long with yellow spots
Which tie with little bows,
Each one has got a purple beard
Which reaches to his toes.

Their eyes are small, their mouths are thin,
Their teeth are large and green,
They really are the funniest men
That I have ever seen.

THE PRINCESS WAI

High in the purple mountains
Of magical, far Cathay
Lives a beautiful little Lady
Whose name is Princess Wai.

Her home is a golden palace
In a garden of scarlet flowers,
Where nightingales pour out their songs
All through her dreaming hours.

Sometimes when the moon is shining
On the silver mulberry trees,
And the garden is lit with lanterns
That swing in the scented breeze.

The Emperor and the Empress
Sit out on their peacock throne
To watch their little daughter
As she dances there alone:

Dancing alone in the moonlight
On the soft, warm, velvet grass,
And curtseying to the peacock throne
As she sways and turns to pass.

Then she swirls like a lovely blossom
That falls from the cherry tree,
And the Empress claps her jewelled hands
And the Emperor shouts with glee.

And the nightingale bursts out singing
And the trees swing to and fro
As the dancing Princess passes
In the yellow lanterns' glow.

And in that wonderful garden
The flowers all turn and say,
"Indeed, there is not one of us
Like our beautiful Princess Wai."

THE DARK, DARK WOOD

The moonlight shines on the dark, dark wood,
      The owls are hooting,
      The stoats are hunting,
      The bats are flying,
And it's full of mystery in the dark, dark wood.

The moonlight shines on the dark, dark wood,
      The gnomes dig and delve,
      Witches cast their spells,
      Giants in castles dwell,
And it's full of wickedness in the dark, dark wood.

The moonlight shines on the dark, dark wood,
      Faces are peering,
      Branches are blowing,
      Grasses are whistling,
And it's full of enchantment, the dark, dark wood.

THE ENCHANTED WOOD

The enchanted wood is large and dark
    And full of mysterious things,
Of imps and pixies, gnomes and elves
    And glittering fairy rings.

Inside the wood a giant lives,
    As tall as the highest oak,
He takes large steps that echo far
    And frighten the fairy folk.

Two dragons creep within the woods,
    Both covered with silvery scales.
Around they spurt their fiery breath,
    While they waggle their swishing tails.

A funny house is in the woods.
    'Tis the home of an ugly witch
Who all day long makes magic spells,
    In a cauldron as black as pitch.

The trees of the enchanted wood
    Rise up to the sunny blue skies.
They hide the secrets of the woods
    From inquisitive human eyes.

THE HIDDEN CITY

There is a park just near to me
    Where I go after school,
And just beyond the roundabouts
    There lies a lily pool.

Sometimes I sit and gaze in it
   (So very quietly though)
And often think that I can see
A city down below.

There is a cold, dark castle there
   Standing straight and tall;
It lies far down beneath the rocks
Quite hidden from us all.

There is a knight in armour, too,
   Who's clad in bright chain-mail
That glistens in the shadows there
Like silver fishes' scales.

I haven't even seen her yet
   But there's a witch I'm sure,
I've also glimpsed the fairy prince
Quite near the castle door.

He's not like any normal prince;
   That wicked witch is bad,
She's changed him to a slimy frog
To make the princess sad.

The princess in her golden gown
   Sits by a lily flower,
Perhaps the knight will fight the witch
And free them from her power.

I wonder if they know I'm here,
   I wonder if they see.
Alas, no ripple stirs the pond,
They haven't noticed me.

THE WHITE UNICORN

When the king went a-riding
On a fresh and dewy morn,
He found an elfin creature,
A milk-white unicorn.

Beneath the shady branches
Of a wild and secret wood,
By a stream of clear green water,
The elfin creature stood.

His coat was white as hawthorn,
Silver his hoofs and horn;
The king cried "Leave your forest,
Enchanted Unicorn!

"I'll house you in a stable
With a stall of beaten gold,
And a rug of royal purple
To keep you from the cold."

Tossing his head so proudly,
The elfin creature spoke:
"I feed on silver lichens
That hang upon the oak.

"Better than royal stable,
With golden stall and corn,
I love the wild green forest,
And the glade where I was born."

He leaped into the water,
Swift, lovely as a dream,
And his hooves and horn flashed silver,
As he swam the shining stream.

DREAM TREASURE

My bed is a ship, and I sail each night
Through a sea of sleep to a land of delight.
There's a beach of white sand washed by tropical seas,
And palm trees that whisper and nod in the breeze.
There are monkeys that chatter and peer and play,
And the screeching of parrots is heard the whole day.
I've a map, with a cross, that says, "Treasure is here!"
As I dig I keep watch in case pirates are near.
At last my spade strikes against metal or wood,
And I've found an old chest as the map said I should.
It has great iron locks and is heavy as lead:
Then it all fades away, and I wake up in bed.
But one night, I'm sure, I shall open those locks
And gaze on the treasures that lie in that box.

THE KNIGHT

When darkness falls I climb the stairs,
Then in my bed I lie.
I pull the covers round my head
And close my sleepy eyes.

I dream I am a knight of old
With sword down by my side.
My armour gleams so in the sun
As on my horse I ride.

Faster and faster we gallop along
Past castles tall and grey,
And then we slow down to a trot
As through a wood we stray.

Beneath the trees I see a cave
And hear a frightening roar,
I see a dragon huge and fierce
As t'ward the cave I draw.

I tremble as I grasp my sword,
Then climb down from my horse.
The dragon fades and I awake.
    was a dream, of course.

INDEX

TRUNK AND HEAD MOVEMENTS

RELAXATION

Many other poems include relaxation.

WHOLE BODY MOVEMENTS

CHARACTERISATION AND SEQUENCE

VARIETIES OF MOVEMENT